The Reluctant Ally

KARL A. ROIDER, JR.

THE RELUCTANT ALLY

Austria's Policy in the Austro-Turkish War, 1737–1739

Louisiana State University Press
BATON ROUGE

For my wife, Sue

ISBN 0–8071–0237–7
Library of Congress Catalog Card Number 72–79336
Copyright © 1972 by Louisiana State University Press
All rights reserved
Manufactured in the United States of America
Printed by Kingsport Press, Kingsport, Tennessee
Designed by Dwight Agner

Preface

      Austria's policies in the Austro-Russian-Turkish war of 1737–1739 have never received adequate attention from historians of eighteenth-century Europe. For most scholars this struggle assumes a minor role in the confusing events of the 1720s and 1730s, all of which in turn are overshadowed by the War of the Spanish Succession that preceded them and the War of the Austrian Succession that followed. And yet, this war marked the end of Habsburg expansion into the Balkan peninsula for more than a century, witnessed the first European interest in the fate of the declining Ottoman Empire, and forged the Austro-Russian alliance that became a common feature of European diplomacy until the mid-nineteenth century.

      This study focuses primarily on the diplomatic aspects of that conflict, especially the reasons for Vienna's involvement, the impact of military events on its policy decisions, and its motives for remaining in the conflict despite serious military difficulties. Furthermore, as part of these specific concerns, it also sheds light on certain diplomatic problems of a timeless nature, such as the organizing and conducting of peace talks and the inherent vexations of relations between allied powers. Overall it offers not only the relation of a particular series of happenings, but an illustration of the challenges of war and diplomacy in eighteenth-century Europe.

The richest collection of manuscripts concerning Austria's policy in the war of 1737–1739 was found in the *Haus-Hof- und Staatsarchiv* in Vienna. In addition to the minutes of the meetings of the decision-making bodies in the government and the ambassadorial reports and instructions, this archive contains many private letters of observation, notes of envoys, and correspondence between non-Austrian individuals. Thanks to the interest of the Austrian Cultural Institute in New York City and to the generosity of the Austrian government, I spent nine months working in this archive, the Austrian National Library, and the library of the University of Vienna, and I am grateful to the staffs of these institutions for their help and courtesy.

Concerning the spelling and use of personal names, I used the English spelling form wherever possible, and, for place names, employed the *National Geographic Atlas* as my guide unless general usage dictated otherwise, as in the case of Passarowitz, whose form is more familiar to American scholars than the Serbian Požarevac. Also, throughout the work, I use Austria and Habsburg Empire interchangeably, regarding both as terms adequate to distinguish the lands of the House of Habsburg. In this work the terms "Empire" and "Imperial" refer to the Habsburg state and not to the Holy Roman Empire, unless otherwise designated.

Numerous individuals assisted me in the various stages of this study, but I would especially like to thank Dr. Walter Leitsch of the University of Vienna for his aid in the delineation of the topic, Professor William Slottman of the University of California, Berkeley, for his penetrating questions and suggestions, Professor Gary Crump of Louisiana State University for his stylistic corrections, and Professor Wayne S. Vucinich of Stanford University for the guidance and inspiration needed to complete this work.

❧ Contents

The Reluctant Ally

I

%& The Austrian State
in the 1730s

In his final report of 1732, the Venetian ambassador in Vienna commented: "Not since Charles V has a prince of the House of Habsburg enjoyed such an imposing position of power as the current emperor. The imperial house seems at its fullest bloom and the fame and glory of the emperor at its height." [1] The sovereign of whom the envoy wrote was Charles VI, Holy Roman Emperor since 1711, successor to the lands of the Austrian Habsburgs, and ruler of a far-flung empire stretching from Silesia in the north to Sicily in the south and from Transylvania in the east to the Austrian Netherlands in the west. When the Venetian envoy offered his glowing assessment, this realm was enjoying a relatively long period of tranquility, earned after decades of intense battle for both security and conquest. From the great siege of Vienna in 1683 to the Peace of Passarowitz in 1718, only three years passed when the House of Habsburg was not at war with either or both of its two greatest enemies, France

1 Alfred von Arneth, "Die Relationen der Botschafter Venedigs über Österreich im achtzehnten Jahrhundert," *Fontes Rerum Austriacarum*, XXII (1863), 27.

and the Ottoman Empire. From these struggles Austria had emerged victorious; not only had it thwarted Louis XIV's bid to become master of Europe, it had also thrown the Turks deep into the Balkan Peninsula and annexed substantial amounts of territory all over eastern, southern, and western Europe. This empire, however, did not represent a unified, consolidated state in the modern sense of the term, but a variety of lands, each with its own customs, traditions, and laws, held together largely by their subjection to a single ruling family, the Habsburgs.

During the last of these mighty conflicts, the Turkish war of 1716–1718, Austria had acquired an extensive but poor stretch of land in southeastern Europe, including the Banat of Timişoara (Temesvár), northern Siberia, Little Wallachia (west of the Aluta River), and the mighty fortress-city of Belgrade, key to the lower Danube River valley.[2] Situated on both banks of the Danube, these rolling, forested lands constituted a formidable buffer between the Ottoman and Habsburg possessions and a strategic base from which the Austrians could launch attacks into the Balkans.

Because of the size and military value of these lands, the emperor, on the advice of his brilliant commander in chief, Prince Eugene of Savoy, declared them "newly acquired" (*neoacquisita*) and thus directly subject to the crown without the privileges generally allowed local landed interests.[3] To administer these territories, Charles appointed two commissions, one for the Banat and one for Serbia, and two military governors, Count Florimund Mercy and Duke Alexander Württemberg, all of which were directly responsible to a joint board made up of officers from the ministry of war

2 For a published copy of the Treaty of Passarowitz, which ended this war, see Gabriel Noradounghian, *Recueil d'actes internationaux de l'empire Ottoman, 1300–1789* (Paris, 1897), 208–20.

3 Josef Kallbrunner, *Das kaiserliche Banat: Einrichtung und Entwicklung des Banats bis 1739* (Munich, 1958), 15.

(*Hofkriegsrat*) and the ministry of finance (*Hofkammer*).[4] Admittedly this experiment in direct rule did not produce astonishing improvements, partly because the *Hofkriegsrat* and *Hofkammer* each jealously opposed any innovations offered by the other, and partly because Vienna did not really judge this region of sufficient importance to invest a good deal of money and effort in it. After 1722, as the question of the Pragmatic Sanction—the famous document securing Habsburg succession in the female line—consumed more of his time, Charles lost much of his early interest in his southeastern possessions. He even granted the Hungarian nobility limited political and financial supervision of the Banat, to the detriment of the central commission.[5]

Nonetheless the Habsburg administration did effect certain changes in the *neoacquisita*, most notably increases in inhabitants of the Banat and transformation of Belgrade into a modern and predominantly German fortress-city. The growth of the Banat's population was largely the work of the governor, Count Mercy, an able administrator who realized at once that only the influx of more people could restore to productivity this war-ravaged province. To settle the empty lands, Mercy attempted to recruit virtually all nationalities, including Germans, Magyars, Serbs, Rumanians, Albanians, Italians, and Spaniards. Only Germans responded in large numbers, the first arriving with the army in 1717 and the

4 Max Braubach, *Prinz Eugen von Savoyen* (Vienna and Munich, 1965), V, 215. The Hungarian Parliament protested that these areas should be turned over to it as part of the lands of the ancient Crown of St. Stephen, but the emperor rejected the request because he determined that this region should also constitute a military base that could be used against the chronically rebellious Magyar lords. Otto Brunner, "Das Haus Österreich und die Donaumonarchie," in Hellmuth Rössler (ed.), *Festgabe dargebracht Harold Steinacker* (Munich, 1955), 141–42.

5 John Stoye, "Emperor Charles VI: The Early Years of His Reign," *Transactions of the Royal Historical Society*, 5th ser., XII (1962), 83–84.

remainder following after the emperor offered various incentives to encourage immigration.[6] As a result the Banat became German-dominated, although by accident, not by intention.

Unlike the Banat, Belgrade became a German city by law. In 1720 Vienna decreed that the inhabitants must be German by nationality and Roman Catholic by religion; all Serbs and Orthodox Christians must move to settlements outside the ramparts to form their own communities. On September 1, 1720, the German residents elected a mayor and in 1724 received the rights to choose a city magistrate, form an honorary militia, levy certain taxes, inspect churches and schools, and regulate the number of inns and hotels.[7] Accompanying the colonists came Roman Catholic teaching and preaching orders, which constructed churches and monasteries and vigorously proselytized among the Orthodox. So many clergymen arrived, in fact, that in May, 1720, the *Hofkriegsrat*, fearful of growing hostility among the Orthodox, prohibited the founding of any additional religious institutions.[8]

In conjunction with the Germanization of Belgrade, Vienna also set to work improving its fortifications in order to make it the key Habsburg stronghold in the southeast. To procure financing for this project, the emperor turned to the papacy, which in the past had contributed substantially to the Habsburg treasury for efforts against the Turks. Pope Benedict XIII, apparently still possessed by the crusade mentality, enthusiastically responded by levying a tax on the believers in

6 Kallbrunner, *Das kaiserliche Banat*, 26–37. The officials tolerated, but did not actively encourage, the settlement of Gypsies, Jews, and Greeks.

7 Theodore von Stefanović-Volovsky, *Belgrad unter der Regierung Kaiser Karls VI, 1717–1739* (Vienna, 1908), 29–30. The Serbian city also received certain privileges, including the right to elect a judge and four jurymen.

8 *Ibid.*, 36; Gunther Erich Rothenberg, *The Military Border in Croatia, 1522–1747* (Urbana, 1960), 107.

Naples, Sicily, and Milan to cover the cost of refurbishing both Belgrade and the fortress of Timişoara in the Banat.[9] Utilizing the funds raised by this means, Vienna began construction immediately and by 1732 had indeed made Belgrade the southeastern pillar of defense of the Austrian Empire.

This region, the Banat, Belgrade, and the Serbian lands to the south and east, provided the setting for Austrian efforts during the war of 1737–1739. Although not considered absolutely vital to the existence of the Habsburg Empire, it nonetheless served as an effective buffer and convenient staging area for operations against the Turks. To augment this territory would virtually assure Austrian hegemony in the Balkan Peninsula, but to lose it would deprive the empire of a defensive zone and invite a renewal of Ottoman incursions into Hungary.

Ruler of this land and the man ultimately responsible for its protection and welfare was the same Charles VI, "by God's Grace Elected Emperor of the Empire in Germany, King of Spain, Hungary, and Bohemia, Archduke of Austria, etc., etc."[10] Son of Emperor Leopold I and brother of Emperor Joseph I, Charles received his first kingdom in 1703, when, during the War of the Spanish Succession, he became the candidate of the allies (England, Austria, and the Netherlands) for the Spanish throne in opposition to the Frenchman, Philip of Anjou. In 1705 Charles landed in Catalonia, easily conquered Barcelona, the center of anti-French sentiment, and, for the next six years, struggled to extend his power in Spain. In 1711, when the death of his brother opened the way for his coronation as Holy Roman Emperor, he abandoned his Spanish kingdom upon the insistence of the British and Dutch, who had no wish to see the same man as sovereign

---

9 Stefanović-Volovsky, *Belgrad unter der Regierung Karls VI*, 22.
10 This title appears at the head of all diplomatic dispatches.

of both Spain and Germany.[11] Nonetheless he retained the title of King of Spain and, throughout the next fifteen years, toyed with ideas to recover his lost heritage.[12]

Describing Charles after he became emperor, Baron Charles Louis Pollnitz, the observer of eighteenth-century court life, wrote: "He is of middling stature and in good plight of body. He is of a swarthy, hale complexion, has a brisk eye and thick lips, for which his family in general has been remarkable." [13] A lover of strenuous exercise, particularly the hunt, the emperor designated numerous court days as hunting holidays and, on journeys throughout the empire, devoted much of his time to pursuing game through the forests. His second passion—after the hunt—was music. An accomplished violinist and harpsichordist, he studied under the great master, John Jacob Fux, played frequently in the palace orchestra, and even wrote an opera in which he played and his daughters danced.[14] Although devoted to music, he also sponsored the other arts: during his reign rose many of the great Viennese architectural monuments that marked the flowering of the Austrian Baroque, a major movement in European art.

11 For Charles's experiences in Spain, see Alfred von Arneth, "Eigenhändige Correspondenz des Königs von Spanien (nachmals Kaiser Karl VI) mit dem obersten Kanzler des Königreiches Böhmen, Grafen Johann Wenzel Wratislaw," *Archiv für österreichische Geschichte*, XVI (1856).

12 Hugo Hantsch, "Die drei grossen Relationen St. Saphorins über die inneren Verhältnisse am Wiener Hof zur Zeit Karls VI," *Mitteilungen des Instituts für österreichische Geschichte*, LVIII (1950), 628. Charles returned to Vienna with a number of his Spanish advisers, who caused much animosity within the government for a number of years. See Braubach, *Prinz Eugen*, IV, 67–68.

13 Charles Lewis Pollnitz, *Memoirs* (London, 1739), I, 230.

14 Hans Leo Mikoletzky, *Österreich: Das grosse 18. Jahrhundert* (Vienna, 1967), 102–103. Pollnitz writes that all of the opera's actors, dancers, and musicians were "persons of quality." Pollnitz, *Memoirs*, I, 233.

While admiring him for his patronage of the arts, scholarship has generally judged Charles VI less interested and talented in affairs of state. From ambassadorial reports of the time and from his almost illegible diary, historians have concluded that, although sincere, well-intentioned, and honest, he was indecisive and unable to grasp problems quickly. Fearful of being overinfluenced, he often ignored good advice and seemed suspicious, particularly of men who deserved his trust.[15] He insisted upon seeing the minutes of each meeting of the Privy Conference, the chief advisory body of the state, but disliked important issues and made decisions only at the last moment.[16]

More recently, however, scholars have qualified the generally unfavorable opinion by noting Charles's sincerely expressed concern for financial and economic problems and his achievements in improving the quantity and quality of business within his lands.[17] Influenced by the prevailing doctrines of mercantilism, he set out to make his empire rich in manufacturing and trade. Industries expanded in various provinces: in Silesia and Bohemia cloth production increased; in the Danubian city of Linz, woolen mills revived; and in Schwechat, a suburb of Vienna, the first cotton plant began operations. In 1718 Charles issued a special patent authorizing the

15 See especially Arneth, "Relationen der Botschafter Venedigs," 22–23; Hantsch, "Die . . . Relationen St. Saphorins," 627; and Oswald Redlich, "Die Tagebücher Kaiser Karls VI," in *Gesamtdeutsche Vergangenheit: Festgabe für Heinrich Ritter von Srbik* (Munich, 1938), 14–15.

16 For this general characterization, see Max Braubach, *Geschichte und Abenteuer: Gestalten um den Prinzen Eugen* (Munich, 1950), 420–28; Oswald Redlich, *Das Werden einer Grossmacht: Österreich von 1700 bis 1740* (Vienna, 1962), 242–43; and Adolph Beer, "Zur Geschichte der Politik Karls VI," *Historische Zeitschrift*, LV (1886), 2–3.

17 See particularly Stoye, "Emperor Charles VI," 63–82, and Mikoletzky, *Österreich*, 114–24.

establishment of a porcelain factory, the second in Europe after the famous Meissen works constructed eight years earlier.[18]

Improving the system of transportation for his new products, Charles built canals and roads, including the mountain route over the Semmering Pass and new highways from Vienna to Prague and Brno. He declared the Adriatic cities of Fiume and Trieste free ports so that they could compete with the old Italian trading centers of Genoa and Leghorn for Mediterranean commerce. To expand Austria's trade eastward, he created the Company of the Orient to carry goods to the Ottoman Empire, and in 1718 he insisted upon an Austro-Turkish commercial treaty to facilitate its activity.[19]

Of his economic adventures, the most famous involved the Ostend Company, created to compete with the British and Dutch for trade in East Africa and in the East and West Indies. Although initially successful the company eventually dissolved in the face of intense diplomatic pressure from London and the Hague.[20]

Despite all of these admirable efforts to strengthen the

18 Mikoletzky, *Österreich*, 156–57; Alfred von Arneth, "Johann Christoph Bartenstein und seine Zeit," *Archiv für österreichische Geschichte*, XLVI (1871), 148–49. In 1725 the Venetian ambassador, reporting on the general condition of the Habsburg lands, praised the fertility of Lower Austria, the richness of the Tyrol, and the success of the mining and timber operations in Bohemia. Arneth, "Relationen der Botschafter Venedigs," 25.

19 F. M. Mayer, *Die Anfänge des Handels und der Industrie in Österreich und die Orientalische Compagnie* (Innsbruck, 1882), 27–31. Although under the "supreme protection" of the emperor, the Oriental Company lacked the right to carry the imperial flag and coat of arms. From the beginning the company had difficulty because of opposition from the Viennese merchants and because the Treaty of Passarowitz placed heavy duties on just those goods the company hoped to sell. For a copy of the commercial treaty, see Noradounghian, *Recueil d'actes internationaux*, 220–27.

20 Although officially dismantled, the company continued to exist as a credit institute and became the principal bank in the Austrian Netherlands until the end of Habsburg rule.

economic posture of his realm, Charles's measures were too few and too sporadic to have a significant impact on the general wealth of the empire. When the Turkish war erupted in 1737, the treasury still had to rely almost exclusively on its time-honored sources of income to finance the army's campaigns.

In contrast to his enthusiasm for the hunt, art, and economics, the emperor revealed much less interest in military and foreign affairs, especially after the general European recognition of the Pragmatic Sanction. In the latter half of the 1730s, he rarely attended meetings of the Privy Conference, at which foreign policy was discussed and decided, preferring instead to keep abreast of developments through the reports of the secretary of the Conference, John Christopher Bartenstein. After reading these reports, he generally approved all of the recommendations therein, made only a few marginal comments, and signed them with "read in full" and his initials. Apparently he seldom perused incoming and outgoing dispatches, relying instead upon Bartenstein's summation of them in his memoranda. Although he followed the progression of events, therefore, he essentially left the formulation of policy to his advisors.

The major role in the actual conduct of affairs fell upon the Privy Conference itself, a body composed of the most prominent statesmen in the empire.[21] From 1734 to 1739, the regular members included the Austrian court chancellor, Count Louis Sinzendorf; the president of the *Hofkriegsrat*, Prince Eugene of Savoy and, after the prince's death in 1736, Count Lothar Joseph Königsegg-Rothenfels; the president of the *Hofkammer*, Count Gundaker Thomas Starhemberg; and

21 The Privy Conference had various names, including *Geheimer Rat*, *Geheime Konferenz*, and *Konferenzrat*, and members carried the title of *Konferenzminister*. Throughout this work, Conference (capitalized) means the Privy Conference.

the Land Marshal of Lower Austria and erstwhile viceroy of Naples, Count Aloysius Thomas Harrach. Often other individuals attended the sessions of the Conference either to provide information and suggestions on specific problems, as in the case of high-ranking military personnel; or to fulfill the requirements of protocol, as in the case of the emperor's son-in-law, Francis Stephen of Lorraine. Meeting at least once a week, these men discussed important dispatches and reports and suggested courses of action for the emperor to follow. Given Charles's tendency to sanction the advice of this group without any changes, its determinations became the policies of the realm.

Not only did the Privy Conference as a body formulate general policy, but the individual members, as heads of the principal administrative offices in the government, also directed the implementation of that policy. Of the major branches in the bureaucracy, the two most active in the conduct of military affairs were the *Hofkammer* and the *Hofkriegsrat*, both collegially organized councils concerned with the financing and maintenance of the army. Because no precise definition of their duties existed, they often found their responsibilities overlapping and, to the detriment of efficiency, periodically engaged in disputes over areas of competence.[22]

The *Hofkammer* assumed charge of providing the funds for the army. From 1703 to 1745, its president was Count Starhemberg, a close associate of Prince Eugene. Earnest, upright, solidly Roman Catholic, and devoted to the emperor, Starhemberg deserved much of the credit for stabilizing the Habsburg finances during and after the War of the Spanish Succession. The income of the *Hofkammer* came from a number of sources, including the emperor's personal lands, treasury lands, excise taxes, the salt monopoly, the tobacco

22 Oskar Regele, *Der österreichische Hofkriegsrat, 1556–1848* (Vienna, 1949), 58.

monopoly, the operation of mines (a government business), the drink tax, and the Contributions of the Estates of the various Habsburg lands.[23] The Contributions consisted of taxes on land and houses in each province, the total amount determined in negotiations between the local Estates and the central government. Because nobles were exempted from such taxes, the burden of paying them fell upon the peasants and townspeople. During the course of the seventeenth century, the practice emerged of using the monies gathered from the direct taxes and the imperial lands for financing the court and civil administration and using the Contributions for the military.[24] Consequently war funds became almost exclusively dependent upon the *Hofkammer's* ability to bargain for the highest possible Contribution from each Estate.

This requirement stood as a formidable obstacle to effective financing not only because the Estates made every effort to pay as little as possible, but also because they, in conjunction with the Court Chancellery responsible for the province, determined the taxable land and supervised the gathering of the revenues.[25] Collection therefore was quite sporadic and inefficient, and the *Hofkammer*, which had to bargain annually with each Estate, was unable to inform the other branches of government about projected revenue from the Estates for any given year. In the negotiating procedure itself, the finance ministry suffered an additional difficulty

23 Christian D'Elvert, *Zur österreichischen Verwaltungs-Geschichte mit besonderer Rücksicht auf die böhmischen Länder* (Brno, 1880), 59–60.

24 Jürg Zimmermann, *Militärverwaltung und Heeresaufbringung in Österreich bis 1806*, Vol. I, Pt. 3 of *Handbuch zur deutschen Militärgeschichte*, ed. Militärgeschichtliches Forschungsamt, Bundesrepublik Deutschlands (Frankfurt a/M, 1965), 57.

25 *Ibid.*, 58. The court chancelleries served as the monarch's administration when dealing with the separate provinces or groups of provinces. In the 1730s four such chancelleries existed, the Austrian, Bohemian, Hungarian, and Transylvanian.

because it could not deal with the Estates alone, but as part of a "Deputation" composed not only of finance officials, but also of representatives from the *Hofkriegsrat*, the *General-kriegskommissariat* (general war commissariat), and the Chancellery charged with the administration of the province.[26] Although, as representatives of the central government, these groups should have cooperated in bargaining with the delegates from the Estates, frequently the Chancellery representatives collaborated with the Estate officials in keeping the state's exactions to a minimum.[27]

Another weakness of the Contributions that affected the Habsburg financial system particularly in the war of 1737–1739 was the special position of Hungary, the largest province near the actual fighting. Land of a powerful and independent nobility, Hungary in 1711 had, after a decade of revolt against the monarchy, recovered many of the political privileges it had lost in the previous century. In return in 1715 the Hungarian equivalent of the Estates, the Parliament, voted to raise 2,500,000 *gulden* annually to support a standing army, an act unprecedented in its history. Grateful to Parliament for this sum and for recognizing the Pragmatic Sanction in 1722, Charles remained scrupulously loyal about preserving this land's special status in the empire and never seriously tried to raise its tax.[28] Thus, even though in the rest of the realm, it was customary that the provinces most en-

26 *Ibid.*, 56. Originally organized by the *Hofkriegsrat* to direct economic affairs at the regimental level, in 1697 the *Generalkriegs-kommissariat* achieved equal administrative status with the *Hofkriegs-rat*, the *Hofkammer*, and the chancelleries, but its duties remained so ambiguous that it became part of a more general war ministry in 1746. Regele, *Der österreichische Hofkriegsrat*, 85.

27 Perhaps the best criticism of this practice is voiced by Empress Maria Theresa in her first *Political Testament*. See Josef Kallbrunner (ed.), *Kaiserin Maria Theresias politisches Testament* (Vienna, 1952), 38–48.

28 Henry Marczali, *Hungary in the Eighteenth Century* (Cambridge, Eng., 1910), 19.

dangered by a war paid the largest revenues to fight it, Hungary was not asked to provide more money for the conflict of 1737–1739 because of Charles's devotion to his promises.[29] The *Hofkammer*, therefore, had no hope of procuring the additional income it would have received had the conflict been fought near another province.

These formidable barriers to taxation produced their suspected result: the *Hofkammer* simply could not produce sufficient funds from the Contributions to provide for the needs of the army. During the 1730s, these revenues varied from 6,143,333 *gulden* in 1734 to 8,124,400 *gulden* in 1736; and in 1737 the cost of financing a field army for six months in Hungary, excluding the requirements of the numerous other forces throughout the empire, came to almost 5,000,000 *gulden*.[30] During wartime the total army needs were estimated at 20,000,000 to 25,000,000 *gulden* annually, far above the yearly Contributions of the crownlands.[31]

To procure the additional funds necessary to make up for the inadequacies of the Contributions, the *Hofkammer* had to turn to other sources of income. Direct taxes offered no help because the bureaucracy, court, and national debt absorbed almost all of their funds.[32] The court was especially costly: in addition to the lavish monetary gifts Charles awarded to his favorites, certain regular expenses were ridiculously high. For example, twelve bottles of Hungarian wine were allocated daily to the widowed Empress Amalia as her

29 The total remained 2,500,000 until 1751. Zimmerman, *Militärverwaltung*, 58.
30 Franz von Mensi, *Die Finanzen Österreichs von 1701 bis 1740* (Vienna, 1890), 747; Moriz von Angeli, "Der Krieg mit der Pforte, 1736 bis 1739," *Mitteilungen des k. k. Kriegsarchivs* (1881), 275.
31 Zimmerman, *Militärverwaltung*, 65.
32 The average income of the direct taxes between 1723 and 1727 was 7,126,575 *gulden*, and nonmilitary expenses totaled approximately 6,500,000 *gulden*. The surplus usually did serve to assist the army. Mensi, *Finanzen*, 654–55, 744–47.

"sleeping potion," and her court ladies received six bottles each.[33]

Nevertheless the *Hofkammer* could—and did—find income elsewhere. The Roman Catholic Church, although a tax-free institution, provided additional money, and it did so not as a single institution, but at various levels, such as the "prelates of Inner Austria" and the "Jesuits of Bohemia." [34] Likewise, funds came from the donations of great families like the Liechtensteins, Waldsteins, and Gallases who, though tax-exempt, opened their coffers in time of need.[35] In addition to these monetary gifts, other income came from special toleration taxes on Jews that could be raised and lowered at the whim of the government, and, in case of war with the Ottoman Empire, from a special "Turkish tax" (*Türkensteuer*), a poll tax levied for the duration of the conflict.[36]

The final major source of funds for the *Hofkammer* consisted of loans and subsidies from foreign states. Although the most famous contributor of foreign income was England, Vienna could draw on a number of other states for money, including Holland, Switzerland, Genoa, Portugal, Venice, Poland, and the papacy.[37] Furthermore, the German states of

33 Alfred von Arneth, *Geschichte Maria Theresia's* (Vienna, 1863), I, 94.

34 Alfred von Arneth, *Prinz Eugen von Savoyen* (Vienna, 1864), III, 398. In 1734, 1739, and 1740 Austria received special loans from various bodies of the church totaling 2,147,350 *gulden*. Mensi, *Finanzen*, 754.

35 Arneth, *Prinz Eugen*, III, 399. Donations were expected from the great magnates. For Maria Theresa's comments on the reluctance of some of the families to give, see Kallbrunner (ed.), *Maria Theresias politisches Testament*, 32.

36 Mensi, *Finanzen*, 337–39, 662. The Jews also had to provide "voluntary loans" at critical times; for example, in 1734 the Prague Jews contributed 200,000 *gulden* and the Bohemian and Moravian "landed Jews" 100,000 *gulden* each for the War of the Polish Succession.

37 In 1736 foreign loans and subsidies totalled 9,231,539 *gulden;* in 1737, 14,498,110; in 1738, 4,867,837; and in 1739, 9,738,343. *Ibid.*, 754.

the Holy Roman Empire often donated funds; and the empire as a whole provided a modest amount in the form of "Roman months," a tax negotiated between the Diet of the Holy Roman Empire and the Habsburg government at the beginning of each struggle.[38]

The greatest weakness of this financing—the Contributions and the variety of special taxes, loans, and gifts—was the inability of the *Hofkammer* to project an accurate assessment of its income and to adjust its expenses accordingly: it simply could not compose a reasonably precise budget. Consequently, in time of war, especially a war in which Austria found few rich allies, as was true from 1737 to 1739, the *Hofkammer* had enormous difficulties raising the funds to keep the Habsburg armies in the field. By 1739, when the Turkish war finally ended, the total income of the state barely exceeded 20,000,000 *gulden*, and the state debt had risen to 99,000,000 *gulden* compared to 66,000,000 in 1728.[39] Upon ascending the throne in 1740, Maria Theresa wrote in her *Political Testament* that she found herself "without money, without credit, without an army." [40]

Despite this rather bleak view of the Austrian financial system, the government still succeeded in maintaining an adequate army in the field during the three campaigns of the war of 1737–1739. Although by no means an overwhelming force, it was able to do battle with the Turks with reasonable hope of success. In this struggle not the financing of the army but its leadership proved to be the undoing of the Austrian war effort.

The second body most concerned with Habsburg wars was the *Hofkriegsrat*, which assumed charge of recruitment, mobilization, and logistics. Presiding over this college from 1703

38 *Ibid.*, 663–64.
39 *Ibid.*, 751, 754; Zimmermann, *Militärverwaltung*, 66.
40 Kallbrunner (ed.), *Maria Theresias politisches Testament*, 29.

to 1736 was Prince Eugene, the greatest Habsburg military figure of the time, whose reputation and genius made him unquestioned master of the Austrian war machinery. During his tenure the *Hofkriegsrat* had nothing to do with plotting grand strategy, preferring to leave major decisions to the commander in chief—usually the prince himself—and the generals in the field. After his death the senior officers outlined operations for each campaign on behalf of the *Hofkriegsrat*, but the tradition persisted that, once in the field, the commander assumed full authority and full responsibility for success or failure.[41]

Within the army itself, the principal officers with whom the *Hofkriegsrat* had to deal were the colonels of the regiments. Successors of the sixteenth-century mercenary officers who raised and maintained their own forces, the colonels were generally high-ranking noblemen who purchased their regiments, gave them their names, and selected their colors. Although originally in charge of recruiting, outfitting, and disciplining their commands without interference from higher authorities, by the early eighteenth century they had increasingly less to do with logistics and had to comply more and more with general regulations regarding matters of organization and discipline.[42] Nonetheless, the colonels still retained

41 Regele, *Österreichische Hofkriegsrat*, 57.
42 In May, 1737, the commander in chief of the field army, Field Marshal Frederick Henry Seckendorf, received instructions to introduce new standard regulations regarding drill and dress. Perhaps the most interesting provision in these regulations required the infantry's wearing pearl white coats, the famous white coat that distinguished the Austrian army in later years. Johann Georg von Brown, "Türkenkrieg, welcher im Jahr 1737 angefangen und im Jahr 1739 mit dem Belgrader Frieden sich geendiget hat," 1737, p. 96. Manuscript in *Kriegsarchiv*, Vienna. Although this work consists of five volumes, for my reading and reference I relied primarily on the microfilm copy owned by the history department of Louisiana State University, Baton Rouge, which does not distinguish between volumes, but between years of the war. Brown himself uses each of the war years as his principal divisions.

extensive powers, including promotion within the regiments, administration of justice (they could cashier officers and sentence enlisted men to death), and distribution of funds.[43] The regiments the colonels commanded officially numbered 3,000 men in wartime, divided into three battalions (four per regiment were created in 1737–1739, but implementation remained incomplete) and approximately seventeen companies.[44] Of the companies fifteen comprised regular troops of the line and two the grenadiers, the latter regarded as elite units and distinguishable from the former by the hand grenades they carried and the tall bearskin hats they wore.[45]

As in most armies of the period, numerous irregularities existed within the Austrian apparatus, particularly at this regimental level. In order to line their own pockets, colonels often sold positions in their units and required gifts of men wanting to marry or requesting leaves for extended periods of time. Some colonels skimped on maintenance money, received funds for men they knew would not reach regimental headquarters until the campaign had ended, and padded their role books with straw men.[46] Such anomalies naturally made it difficult to determine how many men composed each regiment, and the actual number fell somewhat below the strength on paper.

To procure men for the armed forces, the *Hofkriegsrat*, like the *Hofkammer* in financial matters, turned to the Estates of the emperor's crownlands. At the conclusion of each year, the regimental colonels informed the *Hofkriegsrat* of their manpower needs. The *Hofkriegsrat* in turn negotiated with the Estates to determine the number of men each province would supply to the army, and the Estates then apportioned the agreed-upon total among the towns and districts.[47]

43 Alphons von Wrede, *Geschichte der k. und k. Wehrmacht* (Vienna, 1898), I, 61–64.   44 *Ibid.*, I, 29.
45 *Ibid.*, II, 269.   46 *Ibid.*, I, 63–64.
47 Brown, "Türkenkrieg," 1737, Appendix BB.

Although it was the standard method of recruitment, appealing to the Estates was not the only way of finding new men. The *Hofkriegsrat* often assigned a certain number of men for regiments stationed in Germany, Italy, the Austrian Netherlands, and Hungary to find by offering rewards for enlistment. Of the twenty thousand recruits needed in 1737, the Estates provided fewer than nine thousand, the remainder coming from regimental enrollment efforts throughout Europe.[48]

To enlist men the *Hofkriegsrat* supplied special teams of recruiters to local authorities to go through the land looking for likely candidates. Assigned to seek out men "large, strong, and between twenty-five and thirty years of age," these officers had special instructions to enlist none by force or deception and to avoid certain individuals, including artisans, students, and those of noble birth.[49] Under Prince Eugene's direction, there also emerged the practice of avoiding "forbidden nationalities," specifically Frenchmen, Italians, Swiss, Poles, Hungarians, and Croats, because in the words of a regulation of 1722, "they do not adjust easily to our type of comradeship and are the greatest cowards and braggarts, who go from one army to another and even lead astray and debauch good men."[50] Once again, however, these rules represented the ideal rather than the actual, for recruiters often accepted inferior and underage candidates or mercenaries simply to fill their quotas. Furthermore, these officers carried money to reward and outfit their new men; and often, to keep some of it for themselves, they skimped on payments and clothes, so that the recruits arrived at their assignments poorly dressed and ill equipped.[51]

48 Hermann Meynert, *Geschichte des Kriegswesens und der Heeresverfassung in den verschiedenen Ländern der österreichischen Monarchie* (Vienna, 1854), III, 13.

49 Wrede, *Geschichte der k. und k. Wehrmacht*, I, 98.

50 *Ibid.*, I, 98.   51 *Ibid.*, I, 96.

With few exceptions cavalry organization and recruitment paralleled that of the infantry. The cavalry colonels had the same authority over their officers and men, although those colonels of the heavy cavalry were somewhat restricted in their use of punishment because most of the men came from noble families.[52] The regiment also served as the basic cavalry unit, but it numbered 1,000 to 1,200 men, rather than 3,000, and was divided into six squadrons or twelve companies, instead of battalions. Whereas in the past, cavalry troopers brought their own horses, by the early eighteenth century mounts were provided by the *Hofkriegsrat.*[53]

Of the other branches of the army, artillery remained primarily an adjunct of the infantry; in 1734 only 651 men, including 36 mining specialists, were listed as belonging to the artillery.[54] In time of war, men from the infantry regiments were usually trained to assist in handling the guns and then simply returned to their regular units at the conclusion of each campaign.[55] Arsenals did exist for the storing and repair of artillery and other military equipment, but the *Hofkriegsrat* usually employed civilian entrepreneurs to pull the weapons and maintain them in the field.[56] The army also purchased provisions from civilians and relied upon nonmilitary personnel to provide wagons and draft animals to haul materiel.[57]

A unique feature of the Austrian military establishment along the Turkish border was the existence of a large irregu-

52 *Ibid.*, III, part 1, 85, 108.
53 *Ibid.*, III, part 1, 108.
54 *Ibid.*, IV, part 1, 599. Volume IV of this collection, which discusses the artillery, was written by Major Anton Semak.
55 *Ibid.*, IV, part 1, 269.
56 *Ibid.*, IV, part 1, 47–56. Semak lists nine major and forty minor arsenals, excluding abandoned castles used as arsenals, in Hungary in the eighteenth century.
57 During the war of 1737–1739, peasants in Hungary and the Banat supplied the army with produce in lieu of tax payments. Marczali, *Hungary in the Eighteenth Century*, 19.

lar force which occupied a belt twenty to sixty miles wide, stretching along the Austro-Turkish frontier from the Adriatic Sea to the Tisa River. Known as the *Militärgrenze* (Military Border), this region contained largely Slavic peoples who, in exchange for certain religious, social, and political privileges, formed a resident militia to protect the Habsburg lands from Turkish incursions. Despite imperial promises that they could practice their Orthodox faith without interference, these people experienced constant attempts by Roman Catholic officials —frequently supported by the Habsburg government—to convert them to Catholicism.[58] Protesting these violations of their privileges, the *Grenzers* frequently rebelled, notably in 1735, shortly before the onset of the Austro-Turkish war.[59] Because of this outbreak of violence and the position of the *Grenzers* outside of the regular army, the *Hofkriegsrat* questioned their reliability and therefore offered them only a limited role in the war.[60] Four regiments took part in the Bosnian operations in 1737; limited numbers were spread among the regulars in the Banat in 1739; and ten companies of Serbian militia served as irregular cavalry during all three campaigns. Otherwise, throughout the war most *Grenzers* confined their duties to patrolling the border.[61]

Another aspect worthy of note was the frequent contributions of troops to the Habsburg army by the states of the Holy Roman Empire. In almost every war prior to 1737, Austria received reinforcing units from various German prin-

58 For an excellent discussion of the Military Border, see, in addition to his work cited above, Rothenberg's second volume, *The Military Border in Croatia, 1740–1881* (Chicago, 1966).

59 Rothenberg, *The Military Border*, 14.

60 In August, 1737, Field Marshal Seckendorf recommended a *Grenzer* force not be created in the newly conquered lands because these men "prefer robbery, plunder, and stealing" to defending their provinces. Brown, "Türkenkrieg," 1737, 218.

61 Wrede, *Geschichte der k. und k. Wehrmacht*, III, part 1, 82; V, 211–12.

cipalities, and the war of 1737–1739 was no exception. In 1737, 2 Wolfenbüttel battalions and a Saxon force of 8,000 men and 8 fieldpieces joined the Habsburg units; and in 1739, 7,400 men came on loan from Bavaria, 5,000 from Saxony, 4,600 from Cologne, 1,500 from Modena, and smaller numbers from various other German and Italian lands.[62] These forces consisted of regular soldiers who remained in the Habsburg ranks until the expiration of the agreed-upon time limit of their services, which varied from one to three years.[63]

The overall strength of the regular army in the autumn of 1736 stood at 90,929 infantry and 40,084 cavalry, scattered throughout the empire.[64] At that time the main force in Hungary numbered 29,048 infantry, 23,503 cavalry, 10,000 border troops, and 80 pieces of field artillery.[65] Because of the security requirements of the rest of the crownlands, by no means all of the Austrian troops could be employed in the struggle against the Turks—40,000 had to remain in Italy alone—and, by the summer of 1737, when the actual fighting took place, the field army in Hungary consisted of 35,000 foot and 21,679 horse.[66]

As in the case of finances, some mention must be made of the special treatment enjoyed by Hungary in military affairs. Although the Hungarian aristocrats retained their obligation to defend their homeland, they did so not as a part of the standing army, but as a form of *levée en masse* of the gentry in time of war. This form of service having become obsolete with the rise of the permanent army and professional cavalry, the nobles essentially had no military obligations; and, because the Hungarian war taxes were levied only on the

62 Brown, "Türkenkrieg," 1737, Appendices T, V; 1739; Appendix D.
63 During their term of service, these men received payment and provisions from the *Hofkriegsrat*.
64 Brown, "Türkenkrieg," 1737, Appendix G.
65 *Ibid.*, Appendix G.   66 *Ibid.*, Appendix Q.

peasants and towns, in effect they made no contribution whatsoever to the Austrian war effort.[67] Furthermore, even as a
matter of choice, the nobles by and large avoided serving in
the regular army, envisioning it as an old tyrant and enemy,
and preferred to remain at home and administer their own
affairs.[68] As in money matters, therefore, the Hungarians provided far less than their share of military support for the
defense of their southern lands.

The general scholarly assessment of the Austrian army
prior to the outbreak of the war of 1737–1739 agrees that,
during the long period of peace from the end of the Turkish
war in 1718 to the beginning of the War of the Polish Succession in 1733, the condition of the army deteriorated noticeably.[69] Anxious to lower their taxes, the various Estates after
1718 bargained successfully for a reduction of their annual
Contributions, which in turn forced the *Hofkriegsrat* to reduce the size of its forces. As late as 1732, the *Hofkriegsrat*
instituted a major reduction and, in doing so, mistakenly re-
leased many long-serving officers and men instead of limiting
the induction of new, ill-trained, and inexperienced recruits.[70]
After the reduction morale and discipline remained poor because of sporadic drill and payment and because many enlisted men resented their officers, who themselves were often
quite young and untested.[71]

Prince Eugene tried to remedy some of these defects by
abolishing the purchasing of officer posts within the regiments, improving discipline among the men, and limiting pro-

67 Béla K. Király, *Hungary in the Late Eighteenth Century* (New
York, 1969), 70.
68 Marczali, *Hungary in the Eighteenth Century*, 130.
69 Proponents of this theory include Braubach, *Prinz Eugen*, V,
passim; Arneth, *Prinz Eugen*, III, passim; and E. von Frauenholz,
"Prinz Eugen und die kaiserliche Armee," *Münchener historische
Abhandlungen*, II, 1 (1932), 1–14.
70 Braubach, *Prinz Eugen*, V, 222–23, 225.
71 *Ibid.*, V, 231–32.

motions based on family status rather than merit, but by and large he achieved little success.[72] Although interested in piecemeal solutions, Prince Eugene himself appeared unwilling to enact thoroughgoing reforms; he created no officer school and no uniform training manual to instruct new men in the ways of war. Consequently, although he persistently complained about the inadequacies in the army, the prince offered no comprehensive solution to improve its effectiveness.[73]

Whereas the conduct and financing of war rested in the hands of the *Hofkriegsrat* and *Hofkammer*, the business of diplomacy remained the charge of the Austrian court chancellor, who composed the instructions for and received the reports from ambassadors abroad and drew up memoranda concerning foreign problems for the consideration of the Privy Conference. Curiously, however, one foreign envoy with whom he did not correspond was the Austrian minister to the Ottoman Empire, who sent his dispatches to and received his orders from the president of the *Hofkriegsrat*. The reason for this practice lay in Constantinople's refusal to recognize any power equal to the great sultan, an insistence that prevented Austria from dealing with Turkey through normal diplomatic channels. Vienna did enjoy one small advantage in its relations with the Ottomans: the fastest and most reliable postal route to Constantinople from all the European capitals, including St. Petersburg, passed through Vienna, thereby making it possible for the Austrian officials to intercept much of the correspondence *en route* to and from the Turkish capital. Although the origins of a deciphering bureau are obscure, by 1734 at least ten people were employed to hold and read letters passing through the city.[74] Consequently, from the

72 *Ibid.;* Frauenholz, "Prinz Eugen," 4–7.

73 Braubach, *Prinz Eugen*, IV, 116.

74 Franz Stix, "Zur Geschichte und Organisation der Wiener geheimen Ziffernkanzlei," *Mitteilungen des Instituts für österreichische Geschichtsforschung*, LI (1937), 149.

messages waylaid and decoded by this office, the chancellor received at least some hints of the other powers' policies toward the Turks.

In the 1730s the chancellor's office belonged to Count Sinzendorf, who, like Starhemberg and Prince Eugene, had won his post during the War of the Spanish Succession and held it until his death in 1742. A lover of the good life and an adroit conversationalist, Sinzendorf earned a reputation for maintaining one of the best salons in Vienna.[75] By the time of the war of 1737–1739, however, he had lost much of his enthusiasm for affairs of state and no longer seemed interested in the day-by-day arrival of reports and departure of instructions. Preferring the niceties and pleasures of Viennese society, he voluntarily gave up many of his duties and consequently enjoyed much less influence than he had in the past.

As Sinzendorf slowly withdrew from the toils of office, the individual who assumed responsibility for Habsburg diplomacy was the secretary of the Privy Conference and influential servant of the emperor, John Christopher Bartenstein. Son of a professor at the University of Strassburg and student of German law, in 1712 Bartenstein had decided to forego the teaching career planned for him by his father and to enter government service.[76] Initially undecided whether to join the French or Austrian administration, he finally chose Austria because he believed his knowledge of German law would be more useful there and that his German name and background would increase his chances for promotion.[77] Regarding his

75 Pollnitz, *Mémoirs*, I, 241.

76 Although most of the adult males in Bartenstein's family taught in Strassburg, two of his uncles had entered government service, therefore he did not violate family custom altogether. Max Braubach, "Johann Christoph Bartensteins Herkunft und Anfänge," *Mitteilungen des Instituts für österreichische Geschichtsforschung*, LXI (1953), 110, 131.

77 *Ibid.*, 131; Friedrich Walter, *Paladine der Kaiserin* (Vienna, 1959), 13.

Protestant faith as the sole hindrance to his advancement, he converted to Roman Catholicism in 1714, but only after intense meditation.[78]

This young man entered Habsburg service in 1714 and three years later became government adviser (*Regierungsrat*) for Lower Austria, a post which often led to higher offices within the Habsburg bureaucracy. In 1725 he won his first major promotion when he married the widowed Maria Cordula Beintema, whose influential brother secured for him the important job of assisting the secretary of the Privy Conference, Baron Buol. Buol, seriously ill at the time, was within a year incapable of performing his duties and in 1727 Bartenstein succeeded him at his post.[79]

As secretary of the Privy Conference, Bartenstein filled an office that placed him in a strategic position at the top level of Habsburg government. He attended all of the Conference meetings, took notes, and composed the minutes for the emperor's perusal. Because Charles rarely attended the meetings, the ambitious secretary could include his own opinions and suggestions in his minutes and thus hope to influence the emperor and determine policy.

In his new role, Bartenstein first won the emperor's attention during the winter of 1727–1728, when the Conference was searching for a way to annul the first Treaty of Vienna without precipitating a conflict with Spain. This agreement,

78 Braubach notes that a number of Protestants and converted Protestants held important posts in Vienna, including Field Marshal Seckendorf, commander of the army in 1737; the Empress Elizabeth Christine; Bartenstein; General Samuel von Schmettau, commander of Belgrade in 1739; and Prince Joseph Frederick Sachsen-Hildburghausen, the young, influential favorite of the emperor. Max Braubach, "Eine Satire auf den Wiener Hof aus den letzten Jahren Kaiser Karls VI," *Mitteilungen des Instituts für österreichische Geschichtsforschung*, LIII (1934), 74.

79 Josef Hrazky, "Johann Christoph Bartenstein, der Staatsmann und Erzieher," *Mitteilungen des österreichischen Staatsarchivs*, XI (1958), 230.

concluded in 1725, provided for an alliance between Vienna and Madrid, sealed by the double marriage of the sons of Philip V of Spain to two daughters of Charles VI. At first enthusiastic about this union, the emperor had encountered strong disapproval from the other European powers that had convinced him to withdraw from it. In the search for a formal way to void the treaty, Bartenstein found a loophole in the wording, which read "two of the three" archduchesses would wed the Spanish princes. The youngest of Charles's daughters having died since 1725, the secretary pointed out to the emperor and the Conference that, because only two, not "two of the three," girls remained, the marriage contract was no longer binding.[80] Such arguments pleased Charles, who delighted in the tedium of legal debate, and soon he began conferring with Bartenstein on numerous questions of policy.

From that time Bartenstein's influence grew steadily. Blunt and aggressive, he spoke out regularly at meetings of the Conference, even though his position gave him no right to do so. The regular members, all great noblemen, intensely disliked this parvenu but hesitated to silence him because of Charles's attachment to him. Count Frederick Charles Schönborn, the former imperial chancellor, complained that the emperor took away his post in 1734 after he had told the secretary that "his function was to write, not to speak." [81] Königsegg almost experienced the same fate when he admonished Charles to leave military affairs to his generals and not to his clerks.[82]

Bartenstein's greatest interest and influence centered on

80 *Ibid.*, 231.
81 Arneth, "Johann Christoph Bartenstein," 18–19.
82 *Ibid.*, 23. Sautai claims that Starhemberg often told Charles, "Bartenstein is no minister, but only a clerk," and warned him not to heed the secretary's advice. Nonetheless Starhemberg sided with Bartenstein on most issues. Maurice Sautai, *Les préliminaires de la guerre de la succession d'Autriche* (Paris, 1907), 465.

foreign relations. Although the Conference determined general policy and Sinzendorf officially assumed charge of negotiating important agreements, the secretary composed the Conference's recommendations to the emperor and the daily instructions to the Habsburg ministers abroad; by doing so, he provided the subtle inflections that guided the implementation of the general orders. Soon the foreign envoys in Vienna recognized the importance of this unseemly commoner and began to seek his favor. In 1737 Paris advised the French minister at the Habsburg court that "the Baron von Bartenstein has such great influence over the Emperor that nothing can be done without his consultation and approval." [83] Despite the need to court him, the ambassadors found his blunt nature as offensive as did the Austrian aristocrats. His sharp, sarcastic, and disrespectful tone once prompted the Prussian representative to remark, "In one word, he is a small, pedantic schoolmaster." [84] Nonetheless the secretary possessed such authority that even the Prussian went to him with his inquiries and requests.

In the 1730's Bartenstein, more than any other minister, influenced the course of Austria's foreign affairs. He received the dispatches from the Austrian ministers abroad, analyzed them, and offered his judgments of them to the Conference. Further, he expressed his opinion about what course of action the councillors should take, wrote up the Conference's conclusions for the emperor's analysis, advised the emperor on the acceptability of the Conference's determinations, and,

83 Instructions to Mirepoix, December 11, 1737, in *Recueil des instructions données aux ambassadeurs et ministres de France depuis les traités de Westphalie jusqu'à la révolution française*, I, 261, hereinafter cited as *Recueil des instructions*.

84 Walter, *Paladine der Kaiserin*, 16. The instructions to Mirepoix reveal Bartenstein's contempt for status: "Bartenstein hates the Papal Nuncio and rarely lets a day go by without taking the opportunity to ridicule him." Instructions to Mirepoix, December 11, 1737, *Recueil des instructions*, I, 272.

finally, transformed the decisions into instructions for the envoys abroad. At every step in the formulation of policy, Bartenstein was able to interject his own ideas and affect the course of development.[85] Despite his passion for foreign relations, his one weakness seemed to have been that, in the massive amount of day-to-day correspondence, he often lost touch with the central issues at hand. Almost too enthusiastic in his work, his love of detail sometimes clouded his understanding of the general thrust of events. As one historian commented: "His plans lacked that great line. He was more of a man who each day thought of tomorrow, but not the day after tomorrow." [86] Whatever his shortcomings, throughout his life Bartenstein remained totally devoted to the House of Habsburg. Incorruptible, loyal, and trustworthy, he never put his own interests above those of his master.

This general view of the Habsburg governmental structure in the 1730s underscores the opinion that numerous weaknesses existed within it and that certain reforms were indeed necessary to improve it, especially in the realms of finance and the military. But in the war of 1737–1739, victory did not depend as much on the institutions themselves as it did on the men who governed them. These men—Charles VI, Starhemberg, Sinzendorf, Königsegg, Harrach, and Bartenstein—shared the responsibility for formulating foreign policy and conducting military affairs; they examined and discussed

85 Only Hrazky argues against the assumption that by 1733 Bartenstein held the reins of foreign affairs. The emperor alone determined policy, Hrazky maintains, and the secretary only seems in control because he knew exactly Charles's wishes. "Invaluable as a designer of always new means of intelligence and suggestions for negotiations, Bartenstein was above all the only one who always knew exactly what the Emperor wanted, often before the Emperor himself, who, limited and plagued by self-criticism, only found a way out of the labyrinth of his own breast with difficulty. Then was the secretary the sensitive spokesman of his wishes and midwife of his decisions." Hrazky, "Johann Christoph Bartenstein," 234.

86 Walter, *Paladine der Kaiserin*, 18.

events and determined the course of action the empire took. The conclusions reached during the struggle reflected their collective judgment on the capabilities and needs of Austria, and the monarchy's success or failure depended on the ability of these men to translate their decisions into action.

II

❦ Diplomatic
Background

Austria's involvement in the Turkish war of 1737–1739 had its roots in a treaty of alliance, concluded between Austria and Russia on August 6, 1726. A mutual defense pact, the treaty provided for the loan of 20,000 infantry and 10,000 cavalry from one ally to the other in case of attack by a foreign power.[1] When signed, this accord had nothing to do with the Ottoman Empire, but originated in a fear held by both parties of an impending conflict with Great Britain. Vienna's concern over possible British hostility arose from London's reaction to the Austro-Spanish marriage contract of 1725, which it claimed upset the balance of power in Europe and threatened British predominance in the Atlantic. The British brought together France, Prussia, Sweden, Denmark, and the Netherlands into the Alliance of Hanover to threaten Vienna and Madrid with military opposition should they proceed with their marriage agreement. For some time war between these two blocs appeared imminent; indeed in

---

1 For a published copy of this treaty, see F. Martens, *Recueil des traités et conventions conclus par la Russe avec les puissance étrangères* (St. Petersburg, 1874), I, 32–44.

1727 British and Spanish elements engaged in land and naval skirmishes at Gibraltar and on the Spanish Main.[2] While Vienna encountered British enmity over the Spanish affair, Russia's difficulties with London arose from an entirely different conflict of interest, a dispute over who should govern the Duchy of Schleswig, one of the provinces connecting the Danish peninsula to the European continent. Whereas Britain believed that it should remain in the possession of the king of Denmark, St. Petersburg hoped it would pass under the rule of the duke of Holstein, the husband of Peter the Great's younger daughter and a Russian dependent. This problem of ownership interested particularly the English king, George II, who, as Elector of Hanover, had purchased the cities of Verden and Bremen from Denmark on the secret understanding that the Danes retain Schleswig. To allow this duchy to receive the duke of Holstein would void this agreement and force the king to return the two cities to Danish suzerainty.

Actually, in the eyes of the British, the controversy over this province involved far more than merely Danish ownership of a north European province or the sale of two cities to Hanover. To Parliament it meant a Russian threat to British commercial supremacy in the Baltic Sea. Should the Russians establish trading bases in Schleswig, they might offer the English merchants serious competition in northern Europe. To protect its country's business preeminence in that region, in the spring of 1726 Parliament sent a naval squadron under Sir Charles Wager to the Baltic to inform the empress of Russia, Catherine I, that she must under no circumstances

---

2 For general histories of European diplomacy in the 1720s, see Emile Bourgeois, *Le secret des Farnèse* (Paris, 1909), and *Le secret du régent et la politique de l'abbé Dubois* (Paris, 1909); Max Braubach, *Versailles und Wien von Ludwig XIV bis Kaunitz* (Bonn, 1952); Gaston Zeller, *Les temps modernes: De Louis XIV à 1789* (Paris, 1955); and Pierre Muret, *La prépondérance anglaise, 1715–1763* (Paris, 1949).

allow her warships or her men to help the duke of Holstein secure Schleswig. Upon receiving this warning, Catherine announced that she would comply, but objected to the presence of the squadron as an infringement upon her rights as a free and independent sovereign. Wager, accepting her reply as satisfactory and ignoring her protest, then withdrew his ships from the Russian coast.[3]

These two seemingly unrelated events, the Austro-Spanish marriage controversy and the Schleswig dispute, brought Austria and Russia together in a common distrust of Great Britain. Neither Vienna nor St. Petersburg wanted a conflict with London at this time, but both needed an ally in case of one and each found that ally in the other. They believed that together they could better resist pressure from Britain and its plethora of friends on the Continent than each could alone. Consequently on August 6 they forged the pact to protect themselves from the aggression of a foreign power.[4]

Of particular notice in Austria's motives for concluding this accord was the absence of concern regarding the Ottoman Empire. In the decade of the 1720s and in the first half of the 1730s, the Austrian policy makers focused their attention almost exclusively on the complicated diplomatic maneuverings of western Europe and considered eastern affairs important only insofar as they appeared to influence developments in the west. From 1726 to 1733, the chief foreign problems of the Habsburg monarchy included the Spanish marriage controversy and, after the absolution of the agreement, the Spanish threat to Italy; European recognition of the

3 R. Nisbet Bain, *The Pupils of Peter the Great* (New York, 1899), 93–95; J. H. Plumb, *Sir Robert Walpole* (London, 1960), II, 134.

4 A masterful study of the origins of this alliance is Walter Leitsch, "Der Wandel des österreichischen Russlandpolitiks in den Jahren, 1724–1726," *Jahrbücher für Geschichte Osteuropas*, VI (1958), 33–91.

Pragmatic Sanction; and British and French machinations on the Continent to create anti-Habsburg coalitions, matters in which the Turks could play only a limited role. Having defeated the Ottomans in 1718 and won from them the extensive buffer zone in southern Hungary and northern Serbia, Vienna viewed Constantinople as posing no serious threat to the Austrian Empire, unless London or Paris could utilize it to put pressure on the emperor in some general European matter.

Furthermore, during this period Vienna had no territorial ambitions of any significance, either in eastern or western Europe. Although Charles flirted with efforts to secure some claim to the Spanish throne, after the serious objections raised by the other powers in 1725, he abandoned all such dreams and contented himself with procuring European approval of the Pragmatic Sanction and introducing his economic experiments in his Austrian heritage.[5] Having no interest in southeastward expansion and regarding the Ottoman Empire of little consequence in the important affairs of Europe, therefore, Vienna had no intention of or reason for igniting a war with the Turks during this time.

In another way, however, this union appeared as a decisive step in Austrian policy, for it marked the first time Vienna— or any other great power—had employed Russia as a force in western European affairs. Although Austria had dealt extensively with the Muscovite state in the sixteenth and seventeenth centuries, not until 1697 had it concluded a formal accord with Russia to fight even a common eastern European foe, in that case the Ottoman Empire.[6] That agreement itself

5 Braubach, *Versailles und Wien*, 148. After the collapse of the Spanish agreement, Charles's loss of interest in Spain was indicated by the fall in influence of his Spanish advisers, particularly Ramón Perlas de Rialp. Braubach, *Prinz Eugen*, IV, 315–17.

6 For Austrian relations with Russia before the eighteenth century, see Hans Uebersberger, *Österreich und Russland seit dem Ende*

had lasted only briefly, for just a year later the Habsburg emperor had shown his contempt for it by opening negotiations leading to a separate peace with the mutual enemy.[7] After that singular pact, no western power concluded an official military accord with the tsarist empire until the Austro-Russian partnership of 1726. By this treaty the Habsburg government showed itself the first to appreciate Russia's potential, not only as an ally against eastern states, but against western powers as well, and, from that time on, the friendship of St. Petersburg assumed increasing importance in Habsburg policy.

By 1727 the two crises for which this pact had been created had subsided without serious incident, and, for the next few years, Austria's foreign affairs remained peaceful and the Russian alliance dormant. Indeed during this time, Austrian policy seemed quite successful: not only did Vienna reach settlements with England and Spain, but also with Holland and Denmark and secured recognition of the Pragmatic Sanction from the Diet of the Holy Roman Empire. By 1732 the only potentially serious opponent of the Habsburg Monarchy was France.

In 1733, however, a conflict arose that overturned Austria's diplomatic contentment and put the Austro-Russian union to its first real test. On February 1 of that year, Augustus II, King of Poland and Elector of Saxony, died, thus inaugurating a Polish succession struggle. Since the seventeenth century, the problem of Polish succession had plagued European affairs because kings ascended the throne not by hereditary

---

des 15. Jahrhunderts (Vienna and Leipzig, 1906); and Walter Leitsch, *Moskau und die Politik des Kaiserhofes im XVII. Jahrhundert* (Graz and Cologne, 1960), Pt. 1.

7 Bertold Spuler, "Die europäische Diplomatie in Konstantinopel bis zum Frieden von Belgrad," *Jahrbücher für Kultur und Geschichte der Slaven*, XI (1935), 57–58; Ludwig Bittner, *Chronologisches Verzeichnis der österreichischen Staatsverträge* (Vienna, 1903), I, 92.

right, but by election of the Diet of the Polish nobility. By 1700 this body had become notoriously corrupt, willing to support almost any candidate if sufficiently paid. Consequently royal elections degenerated into struggles for influence among interested great powers, whose envoys liberally plied the electors with bribes to secure votes for candidates who would support their interests.

The Polish succession of 1733 was particularly important to Austria because it provided the opportunity to replace the dangerously anti-Habsburg Augustus II with a monarch more to Vienna's liking. Austria's fear of Augustus dated from the marriage of his eldest son to the elder daughter of Emperor Joseph I, because since that union the Polish King had harbored dreams of using it to claim certain Habsburg lands upon the death of Charles VI. For the last few years of his life, he had constructed the diplomatic foundation for realizing his goal, culminating in 1732 with the conclusion of a subsidy treaty with France and a military alliance with Bavaria.[8] Fortunately for the emperor, within a year after signing these agreements, Augustus died, thus opening the way for Vienna to install a less ambitious ruler as Poland's sovereign.

But Vienna did not stand unopposed in its desire to choose Augustus' successor, because France had no wish to lose its newly acquired prestige in Poland and resolved to support an individual who was at least as, if not more, dependent upon France than Augustus. In its campaign to retain influence in Warsaw, Paris enjoyed two advantages: a strong candidate in Stanislas Leszczynski, unsuccessful contender for the throne in 1697, king under Swedish auspices from 1704 to

---

8 Rudolf Beyrich, "Kursachsen und die polnische Thronfolge, 1733–1736," *Leipziger historische Abhandlungen*, XXXVI (1913), 2. In his interviews with French envoys, Augustus enjoyed discussing plans to seize Habsburg lands. Sautai, *Préliminaires de guerre*, 30.

1709, and father-in-law of Louis XV; and the diplomatic adroitness of Cardinal André-Hercule de Fleury, the able master of France since 1726. Of these two men, Fleury was the more important because he would guide French intervention and determine the nature and the amount of support Leszczynski would receive.

Until 1733 Fleury's overall foreign policy aimed at preserving peace in Europe, but a peace derived from the strength, not the weakness, of France. Later in the century, Frederick the Great summed up the cardinal's character by writing: "This minister preferred negotiations to war because he was strong in intrigue, but did not know how to control armies. He created the impression of being peaceful in order to become the arbiter, rather than the conqueror, of kings. He was bold in his projects, timid in their execution, economical in the affairs of state, and endowed with a spirit of order: qualities that rendered him indispensable to France, whose finances were exhausted by the war [of the Spanish Succession] and by a corrupt administration." [9] From 1726 to 1733 Europe remained at peace, but the prestige of France declined noticeably. In the late 1720s Fleury had tried to form an anti-Habsburg coalition among some small German states, but, after initial success in recruiting Bavaria and the Palatinate, he encountered such difficulties with Hanover that in 1731 the project collapsed.[10] By 1733, having witnessed the rapprochements among Austria, Britain, and the Netherlands, Fleury regarded his country as effectively isolated in diplomatic affairs.

Chafing under this insulation, the cardinal saw in the crisis of the Polish succession an opportunity to reassert French prominence in European affairs. Not only could he

9 Frederick the Great, *Histoire de mon temps* (Berlin, 1846), I, 8.
10 Muret, *La Prépondérance anglaise*, 194.

extend his influence in Warsaw, but he could test the British-Dutch-Austrian friendship and force the German states to respect French might. Choosing Leszczynski's return to Poland as his first step, Fleury sent substantial funds to the French ambassador to distribute among the noble voters and warned the other European powers not to interfere in the election.[11] Then in August, before the election occurred, he dispatched a French warship to carry the king's father-in-law to his homeland.[12]

Recognizing Fleury's initiative as a direct challenge to Austria, Vienna quickly turned for assistance in thwarting the French to its foremost ally and collaborator, Russia. By 1733 the Russian regime had changed considerably from the time of the signing of the Austro-Russian alliance. Since 1726 it had experienced three rulers, an adolescent and two women, the last of whom, Empress Anne, had become sovereign in 1730. Daughter of Peter the Great's half-brother Ivan V, Anne remained in the background of the court during her famous uncle's reign, appearing in the forefront only in 1710, when she married Frederick William, Duke of Courland. Their union lasted only a short time, however, because the wedding celebration was of such dimension that, on the return journey to Courland, the bridegroom died of surfeit just seven miles from St. Petersburg.[13] After her husband's premature demise, Anne continued on her way to Courland, where she spent the next twenty years ruling as its duchess.

When called back to govern Russia in 1730, Anne brought with her, as lover and adviser, a Courland nobleman

11 Ellinor von Puttkamer, "Frankreich, Russland, und der polnische Thron, 1733," *Osteuropäische Forschungen*, N.F., XXIV (1937), 27–29.

12 Arthur McCandless Wilson, *French Foreign Policy during the Administration of Cardinal Fleury, 1726–1743* (Cambridge, Mass., 1936), 240–43.

13 Reinhard Wittram, *Peter I: Czar und Kaiser* (Göttingen, 1964), I, 360.

named Ernest John Biron. This man possessed such influence with the empress that his name has become synonomous with her reign: the *Bironovshchina*, or rule of Biron. Vindictive and rapacious, Biron evoked such intense loathing in Russia that in 1738 a French adventurer recorded: "He has offended Russia; he has stolen considerable funds, and God knows what this nation would do to him if the Tsarina died. His Duchy would be an asylum even less secure for him because he has alienated its nobility and used Russian arms to reduce it to subservience." [14] Despite his close association with Anne, the foreign envoys had little respect for him, apparently admiring only his judgment of horseflesh.[15] In fact according to a military observer at the Russian court, the Austrian envoy, Count Henry Ostein, occasionally commented: "When the Count Biron speaks of horses, he talks like a man; when he speaks of men, he talks like a horse." [16]

Biron did not enjoy the empress's favor alone, however, for he had to share his power with two other men, Henry John Ostermann and Field Marshal Count Burchard Christopher Münnich. Ostermann, born and reared in Westphalia, achieved prominence in the diplomatic service of Peter the Great. A master of both diplomacy and political intrigue, he had survived the frequent changes of rulers and political favorites in Russia from Peter's death to 1733, and under Anne became her foremost adviser in matters of foreign affairs. Ostermann's associate and third of the empress's principal advisers was the premier Russian military officer, Field Marshal Münnich. Dashing and romantic, Münnich appeared

14 M. de Lally to Fleury, September 26, 1733, *Recueil des instructions*, VIII, 335.

15 Lord Forbes to Harrington, July 6/17, 1733, *Sbornik Russkago Istoricheskago Obshchestva*, Collections of the Russian Historical Society, LXXVI, 23, hereinafter cited as *Sbornik*.

16 Christoph Hermann von Manstein, *Contemporary Memoirs of Russia, 1727–1744* (London, 1968), 45.

the archetype of the eighteenth-century adventurers: "Of a tall and imposing figure and a robust and vigorous constitution, he looked born a general; no labors have ever been able to check his course." [17] Like Ostermann a native of northern Germany, Münnich had fought under various flags before joining the Russian service in 1721, where, after Anne became ruler, he won the rank of field marshal and the offices of minister of war, governor of St. Petersburg, and overseer of military reform.

When the Polish succession crisis erupted, the Austrians turned to Anne and these three men for assistance. Most important in this instance was Ostermann, guardian of Russian foreign policy and bearer of responsibility for Russia's allying with Austria in 1726. At that time he had strongly favored the accord because he believed that the interminable wars of Peter the Great had so weakened Russia that it needed a few peaceful years to restore its strength. Convinced that only Britain and the Ottoman Empire might threaten Russia seriously, Ostermann sponsored the Austrian union as the only pact effective against both. After 1726 Ostermann made the agreement the core of his policies and, when Anne became empress, convinced her of the necessity of maintaining it.[18]

Despite his aim of rest and recuperation for Russia, the foreign minister dreamed of achieving the one goal that had eluded his old master, Peter the Great—expansion to the Black Sea at the expense of the Turks. To realize this vision would augment Russian prestige, military might, and commercial enterprise not only in the Black Sea, but in the Mediterranean as well, and would win for him recognition as one of the greatest of all Russian statesmen.

In 1733, just when Vienna appealed for aid in the Polish

17 *Ibid.*, 332.
18 Walther Mediger, *Moskaus Weg nach Europa* (Braunschweig, 1952), 81, 144.

affair, the opportunity for Ostermann to fulfill his dream
seemed at hand. Internally Russia appeared stable: Anne had
asserted her authority over dissident elements present at the
beginning of her reign; Münnich had reformed and strengthened the army; and nine years of peace had restored the funds
in the treasury. Likewise, during this time the Ottoman Empire had grown progressively weaker. After enjoying a period
of success in the 1720s, when it had won a great amount of
land from Persia, Turkey had suffered a serious domestic
upheaval in 1730 and, a year later, found itself engaged in a
difficult struggle with a Persia revived by the genius of
Thamasp Kuli Khan (later Nadir Shah) and intent upon
recovering its lost provinces.[19] In 1732 the Persian forces
ejected the Turks from their newly won eastern possessions
and in February, 1733, besieged Baghdad, the principal Ottoman city in the Middle East.[20] Shortly thereafter the Russian
envoys in Constantinople, Alexei Vishniakov and Ivan Nepluyev, reported that the enormous losses in men and materiel
suffered in the east had made Turkey ripe for attack. Only a
few ships and 20,000 men, Vishniakov proclaimed, could
conquer the Bosphorus and put the sultan to flight.[21]

Although Ostermann rejoiced at the Turkish reverses, he
knew that they might constitute only a temporary setback,
and, at any time, the Sublime Porte might negotiate a settlement with Persia, reorganize its battered army, and strengthen
its frontier with Russia. Even then rumors emanated from
Constantinople that the renegade European nobleman, Alexander Bonneval, had already retrained and reequipped many

19 Carl von Sax, *Geschichte des Machtverfalls der Türkei* (Vienna,
1908), 90; Eudoxius von Hurmuzaki, *Fragmente zur Geschichte der
Rumänen* (Bucharest, 1886), V, 22–27.
20 The Turks relieved the siege of Baghdad in July, 1733, but
three months later suffered a disastrous defeat at Kerkuk.
21 Sergei Makhailovich Soloviev, *Istoriia Rossii s Drevneishikh
Vremen* (Moscow, 1962), X, 377–82.

Turkish units along western lines and hoped to transform the whole army into a modern European force.[22] This news convinced Ostermann that, in a few years, a new more efficient Ottoman military power might replace the present, enfeebled one; thus, if Russia were to strike, it must do so immediately.[23]

To begin the struggle, the foreign minister needed only a provocative incident, and in the spring of 1733 the Turks inadvertently provided him with one. In an effort to assist the Ottoman regulars engaged in battle with the Persians, the sultan ordered the khan of the Crimean Tartars to lead his irregulars to the Caucasus to support the northern flank of the Turkish defenses.[24] To reach their objective, the Tartars had to pass through Dagestan, a province in the western shore of the Caspian Sea claimed by St. Petersburg and occupied by Russian troops.[25] In June, 1733, as the Tartars traversed Da-

---

22 A great European adventurer, Bonneval had served many courts, the last being that of the Habsburgs. In 1728, after a personal conflict with Prince Eugene, he fled Austria and the following year made his way to the Bosnian city of Sarajevo. There he appealed to the sultan for admission to Ottoman service and the chance to win revenge against the prince and the House of Habsburg. He announced that he came "not as a vassal, but as a dispossessed sovereign," willing to help the sultan drive the Habsburgs from Hungary. At first refusing to see him, the sultan had no choice when Bonneval converted to Islam. In 1731 Bonneval journeyed to Constantinople to offer his talents to the grand vizier and to urge the Porte to attack Austria. Heinrich Benedikt, *Der Pascha-Graf Alexander von Bonneval, 1675–1747* (Graz, 1959), 82–83.

23 Mediger, *Moskaus Weg nach Europa*, 161.

24 Johann Wilhelm Zinkeisen, *Geschichte des osmanischen Reiches in Europa* (Gotha, 1857), V, 653.

25 In July, 1732, the Russians concluded a friendship treaty with Nadir Shah, providing for the return to Persia of most of the territory won by Peter the Great in 1722–23. The shah agreed that Russia could retain Dagestan, including the cities of Derbent and Baku, because he realized that Russian presence there would cover his flank and rear in his coming war with Turkey. Hermann Abeken, *Der Eintritt der Türkei in die europäische Politik des achtzehnten Jahrhunderts* (Berlin, 1856), 143–44; L. Lockhart, *Nadir Shah* (London, 1938), 58.

gestan, they clashed with 4,000 Russian regulars near the city of Derbent.[26] This encounter provided a made-to-order incident for starting a war, but Ostermann hesitated to exploit it. Even though the Persians had battered the Ottomans mercilessly, he dared not march against the Turks without Austrian support, because the Porte could still make peace with Nadir Shah, contract alliances with Sweden and the Leszczynski faction in Poland, and subject Russia to a war on all its frontiers. Should these events occur, Austrian help would be essential.[27] Anxious to learn if such aid would come, in August, 1733, Ostermann instructed his ambassador in Vienna to ask what Austria's policy would be in a possible Russo-Turkish war.[28]

Upon receiving this inquiry, the Austrians notified their allies that they not only had no desire to enter such a conflict, but would bend every effort to avoid one. Concerned only about Poland, the emperor had already ordered his minister at the Porte, Baron Leopold Talman, to do all that he could to soothe Turkish feelings toward Austria and Russia. Consequently, the Austrian reply continued, the emperor would assist the empress only if the Porte interfered in Polish affairs; should hostilities erupt over Dagestan, he would offer his mediation to resolve the dispute, but under no circumstances would he promise military support.[29]

26 For details see Zinkeisen, *Geschichte des osmanischen Reiches* V, 654. Shay writes that Nepluyev later convinced the Porte to withdraw the Tartars from Dagestan by bribing the grand vizier. Mary Lucille Shay, *The Ottoman Empire from 1720–1734 as revealed in the Despatches of the Venetian Baili* (Urbana, 1944), 143.

27 Mediger, *Moskaus Weg nach Europa*, 161; K. Waliszewski, *L'héritage de Pierre le grand: Règne des femmes, gouvernement des favoris, 1725–1741* (Paris, 1900), 246.

28 Report of Lanshinsky, September 3, 1733, Vienna, in Haus-Hof-und Staatsarchiv, Staatskanzlei, Russland, Neuere Akten II, Box 224, hereinafter cited as HHSA, SK, with appropriate category.

29 Emperor to Lanshinsky, September 18, 1733, *ibid.* See also Prince Eugene to emperor, July 10, 1733, HHSA, SK, Türkei, 217.

Despite this outright refusal of help, Vienna realized that one serious weakness existed in its policy: if the Russians volunteered their support in the forthcoming Polish trouble, Austria would find it exceedingly difficult to refuse a later Russian appeal for help should a conflict break out between St. Petersburg and Constantinople. After all, if Russia assisted Austria now, would not Vienna be obliged to repay the empress in the future? Although the answer would probably be in the affirmative, the Austrians still could not impose their will on Poland and France without Russian aid; consequently, they could only hope to pacify both the Turks and Russians as much as possible and pray that no serious confrontation occurred between them.

Regardless of Vienna's initial negative reaction to his Turkish designs, Ostermann agreed to help the Austrians in the Polish matter; and it must be emphasized that he did so not only to commit Austria to a potential Turkish conflict but also because he, like the Habsburg statesmen, had no wish to see the French install their lackey on the throne of Poland. Given Paris' traditional friendship with Stockholm and Constantinople, a Francophile king in Warsaw would pave the way for the creation of a French-supported Swedish-Polish-Turkish bloc that could only mean danger for Russia's interests in eastern Europe. In fact, even before Augustus' death, Russia, Prussia, and Austria had discussed promoting a common nominee as a rival to Leszczynski. At first they agreed upon the emperor's nephew, Prince Emmanuel of Portugal, who, having no hereditary ties or associations with previous Polish sovereigns, they believed would elicit no violent opposition within the country.[30] Unfortunately, be-

---

30 Arneth, *Prinz Eugen*, III, 359. The Austro-Russo-Prussian opposition to Leszczynski and promotion of Prince Emmanuel crystallized in the Löwenwold Diploma, signed by representatives of the three powers in Berlin on December 31, 1732. It announced that the signatories would never allow a French-supported candidate to occupy

cause of his utter divorce from Polish history, he also generated no support and soon the three powers had to search for a more realistic candidate.

When Augustus died in February, 1733, Russia, Austria, and Prussia had not yet discovered a qualified aspirant to the throne, but, since the moment of death had come, they quickly settled upon Augustus III, Elector of Saxony and son of the late king. Heavy of body and indolent of spirit, Augustus III shared few traits with his robust father. Relying primarily on the advice of his minister Count Brühl, his Habsburg wife, the Austrian ambassador, and his confessor, he had no independent inclinations or thirst for Austrian land and willingly accepted the help of the three powers to win for him his father's throne.[31]

In September, 1733, the contest between Augustus, Leszczynski, and their sponsors began. On September 1, just as the Polish nobles held their first meeting on the plain of Vola outside Warsaw to choose their king, reports arrived that Russian troops had crossed the border to support Augustus' candidacy. The excitement of the news, the liberal monetary contributions of the French ambassador, and the arrival of Leszczynski on September 8 precipitated a stampede to the camp of the French nominee; on September 12, amid great uproar, the Poles unanimously voted Leszczynski their new monarch.[32]

---

the Polish throne and would aid the Portuguese prince to win it. Martens, *Recueil des traités*, I, 311–24. Vienna refused to ratify the treaty, however, because it provided for the succession of a Prussian prince to the Duchy of Courland should the reigning family expire.

31 Beyrich, "Kursachsen," 40–41; Renaud Przezdziecki, *Diplomatie et protocole à la cour de Pologne* (Paris, 1937), II, 196. The agreement binding the allies and Augustus III in mutual support was the Convention of Warsaw, August 19, 1733. Martens, *Recueil des traités*, I, 63–69.

32 Albert Vandal, *Une ambassade française en Orient sous Louis XV: La mission du marquis de Villeneuve, 1728–1741* (Paris, 1887), 200–201.

In eighteenth-century Poland, however, elections became final only by agreement of all powers concerned, and, in this case, Prussia, Austria, and Russia declared them still open. Less than a month after Leszczynski's victory, a small group of clerics and aristocrats in the pay of Russia met in Praga, a small village across the Vistula from Warsaw, and asked the empress to intervene in Poland. Having troops there already, the Russians willingly complied, and on October 5, fifteen Polish senators and six hundred lesser nobles, protected by Russian muskets, proclaimed Leszczynski's election void and hailed Augustus III as their sovereign.[33]

Vienna hoped that the French would realize the impossibility of sending massive military aid to Leszczynski and would accept Augustus' election, but it soon discovered that Paris had no intention of doing nothing while Austria, Prussia, and Russia extended their domination over Poland. The French could not allow the House of Habsburg and its allies to prevent the king's father-in-law from becoming ruler of his own country without some expression of protest. But instead of dispatching troops to Poland, where they knew Lezczynski's associates would have no chance against the overwhelming superiority of the Russians, the French determined instead to attack Austria in western Europe. There they hoped to compensate for their candidate's inevitable expulsion from Warsaw by wresting some Rhenish and Italian lands from the emperor. To assure a successful struggle, Paris secured alliances with Spain and Sardinia, and, while its new associates mobilized their forces in Italy, marched its own armies into the Habsburg lands in western Germany.[34]

Faced with these threats, the emperor called upon his

33 Manstein, *Contemporary Memoirs*, 69.

34 Fleury coveted particularly the province of Lorraine, and some scholars suggest that its acquisition was the cardinal's principal reason for approving the war. Wilson, *French Foreign Policy*, 251–52.

British and Dutch allies to help him blunt the French offensive in the west. His appeals went unheeded, however, because the chief British minister, Sir Robert Walpole, embroiled in a parliamentary struggle over the excise question and preparing for elections in 1734, had no wish to risk his position by involving his government in an unwanted war with France and Spain.[35] To make it absolutely clear that neither he nor his Dutch partners would aid Vienna, he concluded a treaty of strict neutrality with the Netherlands.[36] The announcement of British and Dutch noninvolvement left Austria in a difficult position. Assisted by only a few German contingents, it now had to engage both the French on the Rhine and the Spaniards and Sardinians in Italy. Russia remained loyal, but its obligations lay in expelling Leszczynski from Poland, not in sending troops to western Europe.

In addition to the problem of facing the French and their allies virtually alone, the Austrians found themselves militarily ill-prepared to fight. During the fifteen years of peace following the Treaty of Passarowitz, inadequate organization, supply, and discipline had eroded the morale of the enlisted men and spread factionalism and lethargy among the officers.[37] Because of the lack of officer schools and regular training, few officers had the experience necessary to transform the army into an effective weapon as soon as the war erupted.

This pitiable state of affairs manifested itself as soon as the conflict began, for in October, 1733, the French conquered the important Rhenish fortress of Kehl, and a joint Franco-Sardinian force occupied Milan and most of Lombardy before the Austrians had even completed their initial preparations. Stung by these losses, the *Hofkriegsrat* worked feverishly to

35 Plumb, *Sir Robert Walpole*, II, 289–90.
36 David Bayne Horn, *Great Britain and Europe in the Eighteenth Century* (Oxford, 1967), 124.
37 Braubach, *Prinz Eugen*, V, 230–32, 263.

get its men to the combat zones, but, as late as February, 1734, it had sent only 10,000 to the Rhine and by April only 24,000 to Italy.

The events of 1734 proved no more encouraging than those of the final months of 1733. Although Prince Eugene commanded the army in western Germany, he lacked both the initiative and the troops to undertake offensive operations, choosing instead to conduct a delaying strategy to retard the French advance as much as possible. Concurrently in northern Italy the Austrians stopped the Franco-Sardinian incursion into Lombardy but failed to retake Milan; while in southern Italy the Habsburg forces abandoned almost all of their positions as the Spaniards overran most of Sicily and in Naples proclaimed the Spanish king's son, Don Carlos, king of the Two Sicilies.

At the same time that the Austrians met defeat and disappointment in western Europe, the Russians had no difficulty fulfilling their obligations in Poland. By the winter of 1733, Münnich had already driven Leszczynski and his remaining supporters into the fortress-city of Danzig, which he encircled and besieged. Despite the effort of a small French force to relieve it, the city proved unable to withstand the Russian pressure and on June 30 of the following year, it capitulated.[38] Leszczynski and a few followers managed to escape to Königsberg in East Prussia and from there returned to Paris. In the meantime the Russians installed Augustus III securely on the throne of Poland.[39]

During the campaign of 1734, as the Russians enjoyed success and the Austrians experienced frustration, Vienna made its first formal commitment to aid St. Petersburg in a future

38 For details of the conquest of Danzig, see Manstein, *Contemporary Memoirs*, 72–83. At Danzig, Russian and French soldiers clashed for the first time.
39 Przezdziecki, *Diplomatie et protocole*, I, 196.

war with the Ottoman Empire. This commitment grew out of Austria's exasperation with the course of the struggle, which prompted the emperor officially to call upon the empress to send Russian reinforcements to his troops fighting in Germany. When this request arrived in the Russian capital, Ostermann instantly seized upon it as an opportunity to secure Vienna's obligation to help Russia in his planned conflict with the Turks. Consequently, when he agreed to send the desired corps to the Rhine, he insisted upon a formal statement that Austria would assist Russia should hostilities erupt on the Ottoman frontier. Desperately needing the men, the emperor complied with this condition, vowing to "stand at the side" of his ally in any forthcoming war with the sultan.[40] With this assurance Ostermann dispatched a force of 10,000 soldiers under General Peter Lacy to join Prince Eugene's army in Germany.

Although Ostermann welcomed Charles's declaration as a firm promise to help Russia in the future, Vienna looked upon it solely as a device to bolster its forces with fresh Russian troops. Not only did the Privy Conference still intend to avoid complications with the Porte, it doubled its efforts to maintain the uneasy peace between St. Petersburg and Constantinople. Throughout 1734 the emperor repeatedly posted instructions to his ministers abroad to dissuade the Russians and the Turks from clashing with each other.[41] Too involved in its western difficulties to consider action against the Ottomans, Vienna did its utmost to avoid complications in the east.

Despite the Austrian pleas that he shun conflict with Turkey, Ostermann now confidently proceeded with his plans to ignite a war with the sultan. To begin the struggle, he needed

40 Martens, *Recueil des traités*, III, 69.
41 Prince Eugene to Talman, in HHSA, SK, Türkei, 211; emperor to Ostein, in *ibid.*, Russland, II, 127.

only another border incident—or merely the threat of one—
and he did not have long to wait. In March, 1735, word
arrived from Constantinople that the sultan had again ordered
the Crimean khan to lead his Tartars through Dagestan to
join the Turkish regulars in Persia. Acting on the Russian
foreign minister's instructions, Vishniakov protested these
orders at the Porte, repeating the argument that Dagestan
belonged to the empress. This time, however, the grand
vizier flatly denied Russian possession of the province, claim-
ing that St. Petersburg had restored it to Persia in March,
and insisted that the Ottomans must occupy it because the
Dagestanis were brother Orthodox Moslems and "ancient
subjects" of the sultan.[42]

When this retort to Vishniakov's remonstrance reached St.
Petersburg, Ostermann immediately judged it a deliberate
provocation and began the diplomatic preparations for a war.[43]
After notifying the grand vizier that any Tartar incursion
into Dagestan would sever relations between Russia and
Turkey, he set out to secure Austrian participation.[44] Although
certain that the emperor would eventually join Russia, he
knew that he had to use great care in winning an absolute
commitment from Vienna because the Austrians would not
likely welcome a new struggle while their old one went so

42 Rescript of a discussion between Vishniakov and the grand
vizier, May 24, 1735, in HHSA, SK, Russland, II, 128. By the Treaty
of Ganja, March 21, 1735, Russia agreed to evacuate Baku within a
fortnight and Derbent within two months and give both back to
Persia. Russia completed the evacuation within the designated period
of time. Lockhart, *Nadir Shah*, 86. Given the Russian propensity for
using co-religion as an excuse to intervene in Orthodox Ottoman lands,
it is curious to note that on this occasion Vishniakov absolutely rejected the grand vizier's contention that co-religion constituted sufficient reason for Turkish intervention in Dagestan.

43 Mediger, *Moskaus Weg nach Europa*, 162; Hans Uebersberger,
Russlands Orientpolitik in den letzten zwei Jahrhunderten (Stuttgart,
1913), 167.

44 Ostermann to grand vizier, July 1, 1735, in HHSA, SK, Russland, II, 13.

badly. His task appeared particularly delicate because the Habsburg endeavors against the French in 1735 had fared no better than those in 1734. Although Prince Eugene held his own on the Rhine, the forces in northern Italy were compelled to withdraw to the Trentino, and those in southern Italy surrendered their few remaining outposts to the oncoming Spaniards. Despairing of any improvement, Vienna had already inaugurated secret talks with the French in March to bring an end to the conflict.

Given such disappointment on the Austrians' part, Ostermann knew that he had to proceed carefully, and on July 15, after informing Count Ostein of the Turkish threat to Dagestan, he unofficially inquired about what provisions Austria would make in the event of a Russo-Turkish clash. Ostein replied that he had no instructions regarding such an eventuality, but added that he doubted any Tartar penetration into the Caucausus equaled a Turkish challenge to Russian interests.[45] Assuming Ostein's response to imply that Vienna preferred not to discuss an Ottoman conflict at this time, Ostermann postponed further inquiries; and two months later he assured the Austrian ambassador that he "would attempt with great care to avoid" a break with the Ottoman Empire.[46]

Ostein's noncommittal reply did not really disturb the Russian foreign minister because he felt confident of Austria's eventual participation. His attention now turned to military affairs, for the empress had ordered a preliminary raid on the Crimea in order to lay waste the Tartar homeland and exterminate those Tartars living between the Russian Ukraine and the peninsula inself.[47] Ostermann carefully avoided publicizing attack so that the army could catch the enemy completely by surprise. His decision proved most wise because

45 Ostein to emperor, July 15, 1736, *ibid.*
46 Ostein to emperor, September 26, 1736, *ibid.*
47 Manstein, *Contemporary Memoirs*, 92–93.

the campaign ended in total failure. Plagued by an early winter, the Russian forces on the march suffered from a scarcity of supplies and warm clothing, and 9,000 men perished of starvation and exposure on the steppe. Even before reaching the entrance to the Crimea, the troops had to turn around and withdraw to winter quarters in the Ukraine.[48]

Despite the miscarriage of this expedition, when word of it spread throughout western Europe, it was no longer a secret that the empress intended a full-scale war with the Ottoman Empire. In February, 1736, Biron informed Ostein of the "inevitability" of the struggle and advised him to tell the emperor to begin preparations for a military diversion against Turkey.[49] Russia had come to collect its debt for the War of the Polish Succession.

48 *Ibid.*, 92–93; Ostein to emperor December 3, 1735, in HHSA, SK, Russlands, II, 13.
49 Ostein to emperor, February 12, 1736, *ibid.*

III

✿ The Decision to Fight

The news of the abortive Russian raid on the Crimea surprised Vienna. Although aware of the growing Russo-Turkish enmity, the Conference had paid little attention to Ostein's repeated warnings of Russian military preparations in the Ukraine, choosing instead to heed Ostermann's assurances that he hoped to smooth over all animosity between his empress and the sultan.[1] Furthermore the Austrians had other, more pressing concerns and probably preferred not even to contemplate an outbreak of hostilities in the east. Having opened secret negotiations with the French to conclude the Polish struggle, the councillors possessed neither the time nor the inclination to concern themselves with their ally's troubles in far-off Dagestan; they wished only to bring their own unsuccessful conflict to a close. The desire to terminate the War of the Polish Succession by no means implied that the Conference wanted to free its troops in the west for a war with the Ottoman Empire. Since 1733 the Austrians had suffered dearly and, by 1735, with their armies fatigued

1 Ostein to emperor, July 20, 1735 and October 4, 1735, in HHSA, SK, Russland, II, 13.

54

and their treasury depleted, they needed peace and refreshment, not more combat. To end this struggle in order to inaugurate a new one held no place in Austrian decision making.

Despite this reluctance to talk about eastern affairs, the report of the unsuccessful Russian attack forced the Ottoman question into the forefront of the Conference's concerns. No longer able to ignore the widening rift between Russia and Turkey, Charles and his advisers had to compose a policy to contend with it. No such policy emerged at one sitting of the Conference, but evolved during several meetings held between the winter of 1735 and the autumn of 1736. During this time Vienna awaited events, tried to determine just what Russia hoped to gain from the struggle, and discussed possible results should Austria enter the conflict. In this period of observation and speculation, the councillors weighed the pros and cons of Austria's participating in the war.

At this time—and throughout the war—the Conference did not divide strictly into a "war party" and "peace party," as is customarily assumed. Those largely opposed to the war occasionally showed certain tendencies to agree with those generally favorable to the conflict, and those inclined to participate in it on occasion displayed marked reservations about joining. In these early discussions, the most consistent opponents of hostilities included Harrach and, curiously, Königsegg, the president of the *Hofriegsrat* and later commander in chief of the army in 1738. Königsegg, despite his position, was more a diplomat than a soldier and had served the emperor far more ably in ambassadorial posts than as an officer in the field. On the other side of the issue stood Bartenstein, who seemed to become an advocate of the war not because he wished to fight for specific territorial or diplomatic gains, but because he was drawn toward it by his arduous diplomatic fencing with the Russians. Also on the side favoring participation was Starhemberg, who, perhaps owing to his firm belief in Prince Eugene's eastern alliance system of Austria, Prussia, and Russia, vigorously argued the need of retaining the accord with St. Petersburg. Furthermore, in these deliberations these men represented not the views or interests of their administrative departments—some might argue that Königsegg, as war minister, should have favored hostilities and Starhemberg, as finance minister, should have opposed them—but of their own minds, because they held their offices as members of great families and servants of the House of Habsburg, not as professional soldiers or administrators. By his birth and by his devotion to his emperor, each felt qualified to speak on all matters, financial, military, or diplomatic, and the office he held was generally incidental to his opinion.[2]

Of additional note in the Conference records of 1736 is the much greater attention the councillors focused on the conclusion of the war in the west than on the onset of the struggle in the east. Not only did they concur that the conflict with France was more important, they also agreed that, even if hostilities did break out with Turkey, the struggle would be short and require far fewer Austrian sacrifices than had the War of the Polish Succession.

Of those arguments pro and con, the most pressing against Vienna's joining Russia involved the losses endured by the Habsburg forces during the War of the Polish Succession. Although the troops in Germany had survived with minimal

2 This interpretation does not of course hold true in all cases, but I believe it does in the discussions leading to the war of 1737–1739. After the death of Charles VI, Maria Theresa's most vigorous complaint about the advisers she inherited from him centered upon their advocacy of their offices and not of the empire as a whole. The principal culprit in her mind was not, however, any member of this Privy Conference, but Count Philip Joseph Kinsky, chancellor of Bohemia. Kallbrunner (ed.), *Maria Theresias politisches Testament*, 32–37.

damage, those in Italy had suffered greatly, and those in Hungary, where the actual fighting would take place, had been considerably enfeebled by lack of attention.[3] In 1736 reports from the southeastern frontier indicated that no musketeer had enough to eat or a decent place to sleep and that the soldiers' health and morale had weakened accordingly. The supply system in Hungary, dependent upon ships plying the Danube, had only five boats to carry goods, and the impact of the Polish struggle on Habsburg finances made prospects for increasing this fleet appear dim indeed.[4] Furthermore, the war had caused such a strain on recruitment that, in the summer of 1736, the new men from Bohemia were described as either "professional deserters" or "boys, too weak to carry a gun." [5]

Adding to this military debility, the war in the west had not officially ended. Although on October 3, 1735, Vienna and Paris had reached a preliminary settlement, numerous unresolved problems made a definitive peace still seem a long way off; and, until compromises dispelled such problems, the emperor would have to maintain a large armed force in western Europe in case hostilities recommenced. In February, 1736, Bartenstein brought this situation to St. Petersburg's attention by advising the empress to avoid a formal break with the sultan until at least the French had ratified a final treaty and some degree of stability had returned to Poland. Should the Russians begin the struggle with the Turks now, Bartenstein warned, the French and their allies might break off negotiations and renew the fighting in the west.[6]

3 Count de Schmettau, *Mémoires secrets de la guerre de Hongrie* (*pendant les campagnes de 1737, 1738, et 1739*) (Frankfurt, 1786), 10.
4 Angeli, "Der Krieg mit der Pforte," 252.
5 *Ibid.*, 262.
6 Emperor to Ostein, February 26, 1736, in HHSA, SK, Russland, II, 130.

Other considerations, however, favored Austria's participation. Most important was the argument that the emperor must retain the Russian alliance even at the risk of an unwanted war. Of all Vienna's allies in 1733, only Russia had remained unquestionably loyal to the House of Habsburg and fulfilled its obligations completely and satisfactorily. In July, 1735, Bartenstein emphasized the value of St. Petersburg's friendship by writing to Charles: "Above all it is certain that, of all our alliances, none has been so rewarding or so perfect as that of Her Majesty of all the Russias." Not only was it the most valuable of relationships, he continued, it was also the most natural, for neither power had any territory to claim from the other.[7]

Despite the secretary's latter comment, the second consideration favoring Austrian intervention was precisely Vienna's fear that Russia would win this war handily and extend its influence deep into the Balkan Peninsula, a region of some significance to the Habsburgs. This concern arose primarily from sources in Constantinople, who reported that, because of the terrible losses received in the Persian conflict, the Turkish army had lost its will to fight. The sultan had already issued orders to all the European and Asian pashas to put in readiness "every man capable of carrying a weapon" should the Ottomans suffer additional reverses on the Persian front.[8] Other evidence of this growing Turkish weakness lay in a number of unusually fervent protestations of friendship that Vienna received from the Porte. Not only did the sultan voice

7 *Nota* of Bartenstein, 1735, in *ibid.*, Türkei, 212. This *Nota* carries no date and no signature, but it can be attributed to Bartenstein because of the handwriting. He probably wrote it in early July, for he refers to a dispatch from Baron Talman in Constantinople dated "*vierdten vorigen monats*," in which the baron implied that he would do his best to disassociate Austria from Russia's bellicose policy. Talman sent such a dispatch on June 4. Talman to *Hofkriegsrat*, June 4, 1735, *ibid.*, 211.

8 Prince Eugene to emperor, February 9, 1736, *ibid.*, 217.

his admiration for the emperor in these messages, he even revealed the names of certain rebels in Hungary and Croatia who had appealed to the sultan for aid in fomenting a revolt against the Habsburgs.[9] To Vienna these uncommon manifestations of good will could only mean that, should a full-scale war develop between Russia and Turkey, the Porte desperately hoped to keep Austria uninvolved.

If the Turks were so feeble as they appeared and if the Russians defeated them with ease, the Conference wondered, just how much territory would St. Petersburg try to annex? From the Russian capital, Vienna had received only unofficial hints of the empress' goals, and these varied considerably. In February, 1736, Count Ostein had reported that the Russians desired only the fortress of Azov and minor border rectifications. But by June he announced that they wanted restoration of the Russo-Turkish frontiers of 1700, annexation of the Crimea, permission for Russian vessels to enter the Black Sea, and some form of protectorate over the Ottoman provinces of Moldavia and Wallachia.[10]

Of all these objectives, the Russian plans for Moldavia and Wallachia concerned the Conference most. Wrapped around the southern flank of the Carpathian mountains and bordered by the Danube River in the south, these principalities were

9 [?] La Lande, *Histoire de l'empereur Charles VI* (The Hague, 1743), IV, 537. A revolt had begun in 1734 among the Serbs who protested an ecclesiastical union that Vienna hoped to effect between Rome and the Orthodox church in southern Hungary. Taking advantage of the turmoil caused by the Serbs, a few Magyars raised their own standards of revolution in the name of the old Hungarian rebel, Francis Rákóczi. Aided by the revelations of the Porte, the emperor's officials captured the leaders and, on April 4, 1736, beheaded four, sentenced seventy-two others to hard labor outside the country, and confiscated the property of all. F. Krones, "Zur Geschichte Ungarns im Zeitalter Franz Rákóczi's II," pt. 2, *Archiv für österreichische Geschichte* XLIII (1870), 75–76.
10 Ostein to emperor, February 12, 1736, in HHSA, SK, Russland, II, 13; Ostein to emperor, June 26, 1736, *ibid.*, 14.

both strategically and commercially important to Vienna, for they controlled the lower Danube and provided a trading outlet to the Black Sea. Russia likewise considered them valuable because they served as a gateway from the Ukraine into the Balkans and ultimately to the Mediterranean Sea. Although the Austrians had no plans to conquer these lands, they also did not want them to fall to the Russians; Russian control of Moldavia and Wallachia would not only cut off Austria from the Black Sea, but would make Russia the dominant power in the Balkans.[11] Furthermore, the Russian threat appeared immediate, for Talman's reports from Constantinople indicated that the empress' army would have little difficulty driving the Turks south of the Danube. If the Muscovite troops took only the fortresses of Orgeyev and Bendery on the Dniester, wrote the Austrian envoy: "All of Moldavia and Turkish Wallachia would fall into their hands; at no other place could the Ottomans stop them." [12]

This concern over Russian war aims reflected a very old problem in allied diplomacy: how can one ally limit the aggrandizement of the other without disrupting the alliance. In this case the Austrians believed that the common enemy lacked the strength to resist the onslaught of even one ally, much less both; and, if Vienna allowed Russia and Turkey to fight alone, the former would undoubtedly drive the latter deep into the Balkans and thus become a major power in southeastern Europe and a threat to Austria itself. Believing that a weak Ottoman Empire would serve Habsburg interests in the Balkans better than a strong Russia, the Conference feared that a common Austro-Russian boundary in Wallachia might lead to friction between the two powers, especially

11 Oswald Redlich emphasizes that the conquest of Little Wallachia was only a fortune of war, not an element of Austrian policy. Redlich, *Das Werden einer Grossmacht*, 171.

12 Talman to *Hofkriegsrat*, June 14, 1736, in HHSA, SK, Türkei, 213.

if each wished to annex the remaining Ottoman possessions in Europe. As Bartenstein commented in mid-1736, "One would rather have the Turks as neighbors than an ally so steadfastly loyal [as Russia]." [13]

Before the Austrians could control Russian expansion, however, they had to discover just what St. Petersburg hoped to annex. After all, it could want relatively minor acquisitions —like footholds along the Black Sea—or major conquests— like the whole northern coast of the Black Sea, Moldavia, Wallachia, and the left bank of the lower Danube. If the Russians asked for little, Vienna could remain out of the war and put diplomatic pressure on Turkey to yield; if they demanded much, Vienna might have to enter the struggle, not to help its ally procure all it wished, but to submit Russian strategy to allied control and thus impose limits on Russian aggrandizement.

While the councillors debated these various ramifications, they learned that on April 12, 1736, the empress had declared war on the Ottoman Empire. The Russians were obviously not going to wait for an official Austrian commitment or engage in any more surprise raids; they intended to strike immediately with all their might. Unbelieving at first, Bartenstein called the move "hasty and unnecessary" and blamed Ostermann personally for rushing into the conflict.[14] Despite the secretary's displeasure, however, the announcement meant that the war had begun in earnest and the Conference had to develop a policy to deal with it.

Because Vienna's future determinations depended a great deal on the extent of St. Petersburg's ambition, the immediate task facing the councillors was to extract from Ostermann an exact list of Russian war aims. In June, 1736, Bartenstein came forth with a plan to achieve that end. In previous Russo-

13 Emperor to Ostein, July 19, 1736, in *ibid.*, Russland, II, 131.
14 Emperor to Ostein, April 18, 1736, *ibid.*

Turkish incidents in 1727 and 1733, Vienna had offered to both sides the emperor's good offices to settle the controversy without war, and, although on both occasions the antagonists had declined, the offer had never been formally withdrawn. When in May, 1736, the Porte proposed to Vienna the removal of the Tartar khan as a means of pacifying the Russians, the idea came to the secretary to reactivate the emperor's good offices to bring the two belligerents together. He did not look upon this maneuver primarily as a means to curtail the conflict, but rather to get some indication of St. Petersburg's goals. A Russian rejection of such an overture, Bartenstein reasoned, would indicate that Ostermann planned major conquests rather than mere retribution for border violations; acceptance of it, on the other hand, would compel the Russian foreign minister to give the emperor a detailed outline of claims, because diplomatic practice insisted that each party in a conflict reveal its full demands to a neutral arbitrator. Either way, Vienna would at least receive a strong hint of the extent of Russian intentions and could act accordingly.[15] As the preliminary step, therefore, on June 17 Charles raised the status of Talman to ambassador and granted him full authority to mediate the Russo-Turkish dispute.[16]

Vienna's offer to umpire the peace negotiations by no means meant that it wanted to weaken the Russian alliance. Even as the emperor announced the proposal to the Russian representative in Vienna, he reassured him that Austria would support Russia in accordance with the treaty of 1726 and even suggested that Vienna and St. Petersburg initiate talks for a joint plan of military operations.[17] Likewise, the *Hofkriegsrat* advised Talman to pose not as a neutral, but as a friend of Russia, and to cooperate with and insure the safety

15 Emperor to Ostein, May 23, 1736, *ibid.*
16 *Resolutio Caesarea*, June 17, 1736, in *ibid.*, Türkei, 217.
17 Angeli, "Krieg mit der Pforte," 257.

of the empress' envoy, Vishniakov.[18] In the same dispatch, the *Hofkriegsrat* instructed the ambassador to tell his Russian counterpart that the offer of mediation served primarily as a device to give the emperor time to carry out "necessary measures without inflicting preliminary difficulties on him," those measures being largely the transfer of additional troops from Italy to the Turkish border.[19]

To Vienna's surprise Ostermann did not simply accept or reject the emperor's offer, as Bartenstein had anticipated, but befuddled the Conference by raising certain questions about it. At first indicating that he would refuse it, the Russian foreign minister cited the proposal as indicative of an Austrian desire to void the Austro-Russian alliance and, in that light, added that he could not reveal St. Petersburg's war aims to a potentially unfriendly power. Then implying possible acceptance of Vienna's arbitration with certain alterations, he mentioned that he could never approve Talman as official mediator because his long tenure in Constantinople had no doubt made him amenable to the whims of the Porte.[20] Even after Ostein argued that Vienna's offer served only to cover Austrian military preparations, Ostermann remained noncommittal, displaying only a strong reluctance to reveal the empress' goals.[21]

The Russian foreign minister's implicit refusal to expose

18 Talman was told to protect Vishniakov because of the Ottoman tradition of imprisoning ministers of states hostile to the sultan in the forbidding Fortress of the Seven Towers. To Talman's surprise, however, the Turks treated Vishniakov respectfully and conducted him safely to the Russo-Turkish border. Talman to *Hofkriegsrat*, May 25, 1736, in HHSA, SK, Türkei, 213. Benedikt attributes this leniency to Bonneval, who convinced the Porte that it could secure peace more easily if it treated the Russian envoy well. Benedikt, *Alexander von Bonneval*, 188.

19 Königsegg to Talman, June 9, 1736, in HHSA, SK, Türkei, 213.

20 Ostein to emperor, July 21, 1736, in *ibid.*, Russland, II, 14.

21 Ostein to emperor, July 28, 1736, *ibid.*

his desires posed a dilemma for the Conference. Charles's assurances that he would abide by the treaty of 1726 and the transfer of reinforcements to the Turkish frontier had made it quite clear that Austria would soon enter the fray; and yet the councillors agreed that no hostile action should take place until they had some knowledge of Russian war aims. To wait much longer, however, would rob the Habsburg forces of the advantage of surprise and permit the Ottomans to improve their defenses along the Austrian frontier.

Abandoning mediation as a tactic to uncover Russian wishes, Bartenstein decided to offer St. Petersburg a direct plan for joint Austro-Russian military cooperation, which, although virtually committing Austria to fight, would induce Ostermann to be less secretive about his ambitions. The proposed agreement that Bartenstein drafted read that, should Talman fail to mediate a settlement within two months, Austria would "make the necessary diversion" against Turkey and persuade Poland and Venice to do the same. In the meantime the empress must put her full trust in Talman and inform him of her claims. In the event of war, neither Austria nor Russia should negotiate a separate peace; and, if the Turks attacked one party "with all their might," the other party should strike the enemy "in the rear." [22] Concerning war aims, the proposal continued, if Talman's mediation succeeded, Vienna would ask only for the extension of the territorial and commercial treaties of Passarowitz for another twenty-five years; if it failed, however, Vienna wanted all of Bosnia, Albania to the mouth of the Drin River, and the Danube valley to Braila. As Russian demands, Bartenstein suggested that the empress should request the annexation of

22 This phrase meant that if the Turks sent their major force against the Austrians, the Russians would invade Moldavia; if the Turks attacked the Russians, the Austrians would march into Wallachia.

the Crimea, occupation of Azov, and restoration of the Russo-Turkish borders of 1700.[23] Superficially a military agreement, this proposal's primary function was to extract a list of Russian goals. By specifically reciting Austrian demands and then suggesting Russian claims that Vienna thought satisfactory, Bartenstein hoped to force Ostermann to reveal his desires. He purposely avoided mentioning Moldavia and Wallachia, but included the extension of Habsburg boundaries down the left bank of the Danube in order to show Vienna's strong interest in the fate of the principalities.[24]

Because of the territorial claims Bartenstein put forward in this document as Austria's possible reward for joining the conflict, the role of Habsburg war aims at this stage of developments deserves some mention. After retiring from active policy making, Bartenstein wrote a history for the eldest son of Maria Theresa, the later Joseph II, in which he suggested that he favored the war originally because it provided the House of Habsburg an opportunity to win some land to compensate for the western European possessions lost in the War of the Polish Succession.[25] Likewise, during the struggle the Venetian ambassador suggested that the Austrian government—which he believed was led by Bartenstein and Prince Sachsen-Hildburghausen—had begun hostilities precisely to annex Ottoman territory.[26] Although the possibility of conquest, as well as speculation regarding how much land would be won, entered into the talk of the Viennese court, the min-

23 Project for a plan of joint operations in emperor to Ostein, July 19, 1736, *ibid.*, 131.

24 The detailed instructions to Ostein regarding this convention can be found in emperor to Ostein, July 19, 1736, *ibid.*

25 Arneth, "Bartenstein," 169. Of this article, pp. 71–214 include the history written for Joseph. The work ends with the date May 13, 1762, the empress's forty-fifth birthday.

26 Arneth "Relationen," 181–84.

utes of the Conference's deliberations and Bartenstein's memoranda indicate that annexation of territory played a decidedly
secondary part in Austria's entry into the war.

Bartenstein's goal, then, was to learn his ally's intentions
rather than to put forth his master's claims, but once again
Ostermann evaded the secretary's thrust by raising questions
about the proposed convention rather than offering to negotiate an accord on the basis of it. Commenting that it looked
like a new treaty rather than a plan for military operations,
the foreign minister mentioned that, if Vienna simply fulfilled
its responsibilities under the alliance of 1726, such additional
agreements would be unnecessary. Concerning the articles on
war aims, he noted only that the emperor demanded far more
land than anyone in St. Petersburg had expected he would
and, regarding his empress' wishes, mentioned that, when
time came to make peace, she would "astound the world with
the moderation of her ambition." [27]

For the second time, Bartenstein's efforts to learn his ally's
intentions met with disappointment. The only remaining tactic appeared to be a formal declaration of war on the Ottoman
Empire and the conclusion of plans for joint strategy that
Vienna could manipulate to contain Russian aggrandizement.
But an official entry into hostilities constituted a decision of
immense importance—one which Bartenstein could scarcely
utilize as a diplomatic ploy. Consequently in early September
the councillors gathered to decide once and for all "if Austria
should take part in the struggle." The arguments for and
against participation revealed nothing new. The proponents,
particularly Starhemberg, cited the need to retain the Russian
union and the ease with which the Habsburg forces could
rout the Ottomans; and the opponents, for whom Harrach

27 Ostein to emperor, August 21, 1736, in HHSA, SK, Russland,
II, 14.

served as spokesman, pointed out the weakness of Austrian finances and the threat of a renewed war in the west.[28]

In the end the majority voted in favor of war; the emperor could not afford to lose the Russian alliance nor could he allow an unrestricted Russian penetration into the Balkans. Despite the decision to begin hostilities, however, the councillors unanimously concurred on one essential point: the war must end within one year because Austria could not endure a sustained struggle. In the minds of the Habsburg advisers, the army was too weak and the treasury too depleted to conduct more than one campaign. Had they the slightest inkling that the conflict would last three long years, they would never have consented to participate in it.

28 Bartenstein to emperor, September 12, 1736, in *ibid.*, Vorträge, 44. Attending this meeting as military advisers were General Samuel Schmettau and Prince Sachsen-Hildburghausen, the latter regarded as an "expert" on Balkan affairs because of his work in quelling the *Grenzer* uprising of 1735 and in submitting detailed proposals for reform of the Military Border. Rothenberg, *Military Border in Croatia, 1740–1882*, 14–17.

IV

❧ Diplomatic Preparations

Despite the Conference's resolution to join the fray, fighting could not simply begin immediately, for entry into war required extensive diplomatic as well as military preparations. The first of Vienna's foreign policy concerns remained the conclusion of an agreement with the Russians to insure their full cooperation. Having entered the struggle to aid Russia, the Austrians wanted written assurance that their ally would not abandon them in the midst of the struggle.

Accordingly on September 13 Bartenstein dispatched to St. Petersburg another proposal for a convention. Approximating closely his outline of July 19, it included only two important changes: first, it provided that either party, in the event of attack from a third power, would aid its associate with full resources rather than the 30,000 men stipulated in the treaty of 1726; second, the pact omitted all mention of war aims.[1] Of greater importance was the latter alteration, which unintentionally made it possible for either ally to refuse to discuss objectives even at a later date. Failing to link war

1 Emperor to Ostein, September 13, 1736, in HHSA, SK, Russland, II, 132.

aims and promises of aid specifically, Bartenstein inadvertently implied that the emperor's army would fight even if the Russians did not reveal their goals.[2] Besides these two major modifications, the only other addition of note was the Austrian secretary's insistence that Habsburg participation depended totally upon Russian acceptance of this projected agreement.[3]

In contrast to the previous reception of similar overtures, this Austrian initiative won an immediate and enthusiastic response in St. Petersburg, for by late 1736 Russia had found itself in severe military and diplomatic difficulty. Having begun with every prospect of success, its second campaign, launched in the spring of 1736, ended in failure. By midspring two armies had engaged the enemy, the smaller investing Azov, a fortress standing at the mouth of the Don River and protecting Turkish possessions around the Sea of Azov; and the larger—under Münnich's personal command—penetrating the Crimean peninsula, the home of the Tartans.[4] Whereas the smaller force took Azov on July 1, the main body proved unable to draw the enemy in the Crimea into a major encounter.[5] Instead of meeting the Russians in pitched battle, the Tartars had chosen to retreat, avoiding their foe and destroying supplies and forage in his path. Frustrated by this strategy, the Russians turned from pursuing the enemy to

2 Although knowing that communications between Vienna and St. Petersburg would prevent the conclusion and ratification of the proposed convention before January, 1737, Bartenstein offered to attack the Turks in late 1736, if the Russians accepted his terms without changes. Bartenstein to emperor, October 9, 1736, in *ibid.*, Vorträge, 45.

3 Emperor to Ostein, October 8, 1736, in *ibid.*, Russland, II, 132.

4 Münnich commanded the force which besieged Azov but, once the siege began, left to join the army poised for the invasion of the Crimea.

5 For the brief diary of Field Marshal Peter Lacy, who conducted the siege of Azov, see Prince Charles de Ligne, *Mélanges militaires, littéraires, et sentimentaires* (Leopoldberg, 1796), IV, 55–56.

plundering and terrorizing the countryside, a policy that culminated in the conquest and sack of the Tartar capital of Bakhchisaray and the destruction of the famous Jesuit library there.[6] By late summer, however, the Tartar planning paid off. Short of supplies, exhausted by constant marching, and plagued by spreading disease, the empress' soldiers found themselves forced to abandon the Crimea and retire to winter quarters in the Ukraine. Despite the lack of actual fighting, the campaign proved quite costly: although only 2,000 men died in combat, an estimated 30,000 perished from hunger, exposure, and disease.[7]

Augmenting the misfortune of its military venture, St. Petersburg simultaneously suffered a substantial diplomatic setback when word arrived in the Russian capital that a settlement had been negotiated between the Turks and the Persians. Before launching their own attack on the Ottomans, the Russians in 1735 had signed an agreement with the Persian sovereign, Nadir Shah, by which the latter promised to accept no Turkish terms without Russian approval. By concluding this accord, St. Petersburg assumed that Persia would continue its war and thereby keep a large number of Turkish veterans preoccupied in the Middle East and unable to march against the Russians. Nonetheless, despite this pact and repeated assurances that he would abide by it, on October 17, 1736, the shah approved a treaty ending hostilities with the Ottoman Empire.[8]

The disappointment of the Crimean campaign and the Turko-Persian peace robbed Ostermann of his basic advan-

6 Manstein, *Contemporary Memoirs*, 99–123.
7 *Ibid.*, 123.
8 Abeken, *Eintritt der Türkei*, 153. Lockhart maintains that Nadir Shah did not break his word with Russia because the Perso-Turkish agreement was a truce, not a treaty, and the Persian ruler never admitted that he had signed a formal peace. The truce ended in 1742, when the Perso-Turkish struggle began anew. Lockhart, *Nadir Shah*, 107.

tage in dealing with the Austrians—confidence in unchecked
Russian success. Faced now with the possibility of defeat unless Vienna firmly committed its support, the Russian foreign
minister notified Ostein on October 2 that he would gladly
discuss a new convention based upon Bartenstein's suggestions.[9]

As the preliminary talks got under way, however, it became evident that the abrasive personality of the Austrian
envoy not only made exchanges difficult, but actually endan-
gered the chances of reaching a satisfactory solution. Although hard-working and diligent, Ostein lacked one trait
essential to successful diplomats—tact. By habitually lectur-
ing Ostermann and Biron on the weaknesses of Russia's foreign policy, the minister soon alienated both Russian officials,
who declined to admit him to audiences and avoided him at
court functions. By no means confined to this set of negotiations, Ostein's brashness endured throughout his tenure at the
court of St. Petersburg; as a result he often failed to penetrate
the inner workings of the Russian decision-making apparatus.
This weakness the ambassador himself recognized to some
extent, for he found it necessary to reassure Vienna of his
value by repeatedly extolling his devotion to the emperor, his
knowledge of affairs, and his sparkling manner, which
prompted him "to flatter even the little children in the
streets." [10]

Despite similar protestations of his winning ways, in these
particular talks Ostein adopted a pompous and condescending
tone that poisoned the atmosphere from the beginning. For
instance, when Ostermann hinted that the empress might de-

9 Ostein to Sinzendorf, October 2, 1736, in HHSA, SK, Russland,
II, 14. By October 2 the Russians had not yet seen Bartenstein's plan
of September 13, so Ostermann was speaking of his July proposals.
Soon afterward, Ostein presented the September design, and negotiations began. Ostermann to Ostein, October 7, 1736, *ibid.*
10 Ostein to Sinzendorf, January 25, 1738, in *ibid.*, 17.

mand most of Wallachia by right of conquest, Ostein laughingly remarked that such a claim sounded ludicrous because none of her soldiers had set foot in Moldavia, much less Wallachia.[11] Accurate assessments or not, comments such as this only irritated the Russians, and soon Ostermann refused to speak to the envoy. As a result of this friction, discussions broke down and no meetings took place throughout much of October and November. Meanwhile in Vienna the Conference, apparently unaware of the personal antagonism between its representative and its allied court, speculated that St. Petersburg's unwillingness to exchange views reflected a desire to conclude a separate peace.[12]

In early December Ostermann decided that, notwithstanding his aversion to Ostein, an agreement must be reached with Austria in order to prepare for the campaign of 1737. Instead of swallowing his dislike and initiating serious negotiations with the Habsburg envoy, however, he authorized the Russian ambassador to the emperor's court, Louis Casimir Lanshinsky, to work toward a solution in Vienna itself.[13] About this rejection of the Austrian representative's services, one observer commented: "Ostein tried to force Ostermann to accept everything he proposed by speaking in a high and commanding tone. Ostermann answered in the same manner and several harsh expressions passed between them. As a result, the Tsarina sent full powers to Lanshinsky to negotiate a plan of operations in Vienna. Ostein has now the morti-

11 Ostein to emperor, October 8, 1736, in *ibid.*, 14.
12 Konferenz Protokolle, November 21, 1736, in *ibid.*, Vorträge, 45. At this meeting Starhemberg commented that "Russia would sign a peace treaty today if it were possible because it has fears of an outbreak of war with Sweden."
13 A Pole and a Roman Catholic, Lanshinsky remained Russian ambassador from 1720 to 1751. An adequate, but not brilliant, minister, Lanshinsky, according to the French envoy Mirepoix, "could scarcely thank his own talent for his diplomatic success." Braubach, "Eine Satire auf den Wiener Hof," 73.

fication to see this affair taken out of his hands and sent back to Vienna." [14]

The speed with which talks were concluded in the imperial capital not only underscored Ostein's ineptness, but also indicated how close the Austrian and Russian positions actually were. Lanshinsky requested only one substantive change in Bartenstein's original draft: that the emperor agree to march against the enemy by April instead of waiting for reports that the Russians had already taken the field as the secretary had suggested. Although rejecting this amendment because it implied that the Austrians would have to begin fighting regardless of Russian actions, the Conference immediately appointed Sinzendorf to meet with the Russian minister in order to reach a compromise.[15] After only nine days of negotiations, both parties agreed that the emperor would attack "in the coming spring," without specifying any month.[16] This solution being acceptable to all, on January 9, 1737, Lanshinsky and the entire Conference signed the convention.

This document assured Austria's entry into the struggle and provided a scheme for close cooperation between the allies to protect each from the whim of the other. By far the most important article stipulated that, failing a peace settlement during the winter, the emperor would contribute 80,000 men to the conflict rather than the 30,000 provided for in the treaty of 1726. After this key provision, the others dealt largely with potential problems arising during operations. For instance, one read that, to keep informed of enemy strategy and coordinate movements, the commanding officers of the two field armies should communicate directly with each other; then, in the event of an all-out Turkish offensive against

14 Rondeau to Harrington, December 11/22, 1736, *Sbornik,* LXXX, 83.

15 Bartenstein to emperor, January 6, 1737, in HHSA, SK, Vorträge, 45.

16 Bartenstein to emperor, January 8, 1737, *ibid.*

either force, the other commander could strike the enemy where it would hurt most, that is, the Russians by invading Moldavia or the Austrians Wallachia. In matters of diplomacy, neither ally should sign a separate peace or even negotiate individually without asking approval of the other, and, should any other European power attack either party, both would cooperate fully to repel the attack. Likewise, should any other power mediate, both would deal jointly with the mediator. Finally, both agreed to keep the convention secret, pending ratification.[17]

Considered superficially, this agreement not only appeared to satisfy Vienna's basic needs—assurances that Russia would send relief quickly should the Turks launch their main force against the Austrians, would defend Habsburg interests against renewed French or Spanish aggression, and would reject overtures for a separate settlement—but also provided formal recognition of Talman's efforts in Constantinople to secure a settlement before spring. But it overlooked two important items. Because the negotiators had preferred to allow the officers to work out major operations in the field, this convention, although designed as a military agreement, prescribed no strategy except in the broadest outlines. While this solution appeared satisfactory in principle, the Habsburg ministers neglected to insist upon an escape clause by which Vienna could refuse to fight if the officers failed to agree on a campaign plan acceptable to both sides. This oversight meant that, regardless of promises of aid, the Russians might adopt objectives that would make it geographically or logistically impossible for them to come to their ally's assistance. Why the Austrians committed this error is difficult to determine. Perhaps the explanation revolves around the absence of military men in the actual formulation of the plan—neither Bar-

17 A published copy of this convention can be found in Martens, *Recueil des traités*, I, 69–80.

tenstein who composed it nor Sinzendorf who negotiated it possessed any military background—and a certain trust on the part of the Austrians that the Russians would avoid such an act that would betray the spirit, if not the content, of the pact. The documents of the period indicate that the Habsburg policy makers gave this possibility no consideration. They expressed great surprise when they discovered the Russians planned to launch their major attack against an objective far from the Austrian theater of combat.

In addition to this oversight, the accord did not define what constituted a major Turkish thrust against either ally. Given the nature of eighteenth-century warfare such a definition could have been possible. For example, when at war the grand vizier usually commanded the main force, thus his presence could determine the region of the principal Turkish objective. If that was unacceptable, the movements of the large Turkish army located at Babadag on the Danube could serve as the decisive factor. If it crossed the Danube and headed into Moldavia, the pact could establish that Russia would be the object of the main attack, whereas if this force remained south of the Danube and marched toward Serbia, Austria would suffer the principal blow. Admittedly both phrasings possess certain objections and obscurities, but at least each could have provided some direction in determining who would bear the greater portion of the fighting. Without such a definition, however, either party could claim that it was encountering the major Turkish resistance and could exhort the other to put heavier pressure on the enemy.

Nonetheless, the convention was concluded, and, shortly after its signing, the Conference prepared to dispatch to St. Petersburg suggestions for the forthcoming campaign, which the Habsburg statesmen had been discussing since the previous September. The most interesting and far-reaching plan considered by the councillors had come from Baron Talman, who had recommended an ambitious offensive. He suggested first investing the Turkish fortress-cities of Vidin and Nish, then thrusting south and east, and eventually forging a frontier stretching from Ruse on the lower Danube to Salonica on the Aegean Sea. Such an operation, he had emphasized, would place more than half of the Turkish possessions in Europe under Habsburg control, excluding only Moldavia, Greece, eastern Bulgaria, and Macedonia.[18] Although Vienna never seriously considered implementing this plan, it does illustrate that a well-informed observer believed that the Ottoman Empire was too weak to defend itself and that the time was ripe for Austria to establish its hegemony over the Balkan Peninsula.

The formally proposed operations—much less pretentious than Talman's grandiose scheme—emerged from a late October meeting attended by all the councillors and several field officers.[19] They chose as their first objective the fortress of Vidin, located two hundred miles southeast of Belgrade. Possessing only a wall with few modern defenses before 1718, Vidin had been transformed by the Ottomans into the principal bastion protecting Turkish Wallachia after the Peace of Passarowitz. The emperor's advisers reasoned that the capture of this stronghold would enable their army to eject the Turks from all of western Wallachia and probably deter

18 Brown, "Türkenkrieg," 1737, 69–74. Angeli and Redlich examined Talman's plan and reached different conclusions regarding its merit. Angeli believed the project militarily sound and politically feasible, but dependent upon speed and decisiveness. Redlich, on the other hand, considered the plan ludicrous. Even to think of it, he maintained, would have required Prince Eugene at his strategic and tactical best and the army at its peak of fighting trim. Angeli, "Krieg mit der Pforte," 218–19; Redlich, *Das Werden einer Grossmacht*, 277.
19 The military advisers included Schmettau, Prince Sachsen-Hildburghausen, and Field Marshal Oliver Wallis. Curiously, also listed is Prince Eugene, who died in April, 1736. Perhaps this error indicates the influence of the prince's "spirit" on subsequent Austrian military ventures.

the Russians from demanding the Danubian principalities as protectorates. After Vidin the Austrian forces would besiege the fortress of Nish on the Morava River south of Belgrade, in order to deprive the enemy of his last base of operations near the imperial frontier.[20]

For successful implementation of this outline, cooperation between the allied armies was considered essential because reports indicated that the Turks, believing Austria a greater menace than Russia, would respond to the emperor's declaration of war with efforts to throw back the Habsburg thrust and to launch a counteroffensive as soon as possible. To be certain that the Russians could provide military assistance in such an eventuality, the Conference recommended to its ally's strategists that they choose the fortress of Khotin on the upper Dniester as their principal objective. If this point fell into Russian hands, the councillors noted, allied forces could act jointly in upper Moldavia and Transylvania and send combined armies to any theater that seemed threatened. Pleased with their efforts and convinced of the plan's good sense, the ministers instructed the *Hofkriegsrat* to select an officer to carry their design to the Russians. Colonel John Leopold Barenklau won the assignment and, just after the signing of the convention of January 9, set out for St. Petersburg.

20 Conference Protocol, October 26, 1736, in HHSA, SK, Vorträge, 45. Königsegg preferred an assault on Nish rather than Vidin, arguing that a siege of Vidin would leave the Bosnian border open to Turkish raids whereas the siege of Nish would protect it. Furthermore, should an Ottoman relief force defeat the Austrians before Vidin, the defiles of the region would make an orderly retreat next to impossible. Even if the siege succeeded, he emphasized, the army would succumb to the malaria that plagued that area. Brown, "Türkenkrieg," 1737, pp. 77–91. To corroborate the war minister, Schmettau mentions that the army must take Vidin quickly, "because toward the end of July, the bad air, which dominates the country, reduces greatly the number of combatants." Schmettau, *Mémoires secrets*, 15–16. In January the Conference confirmed the decision to invest Vidin. Konferenz Protokolle, January 18, 1737, in HHSA, SK, Vorträge, 45.

If the Austrians expected the Russians to accept their ideas, they suffered a rude shock. Even before Barenklau arrived in the Russian capital, Ostermann presented to Ostein what he pronounced the definitive outline of Russian strategy.[21] As its primary objective, the empress' staff had chosen not Khotin —or anyplace near it—but the fortress of Ochakov, situated near the mouth of the Bug River; as a secondary operation, the staff had decided upon another raid into the Crimea.[22] Before Ostein had a chance to comment on this sketch, the Russian minister emphasized that his officers had designed it not to further Russian aggrandizement, but precisely to keep Turkish pressure off the Austrians. The invasion of the Crimea, he noted, would bar Ottoman forces in Persia from returning to Europe, and the siege of Ochakov would oblige the Grand Vizier to use every available soldier for its relief. Thus, compelled to concentrate on the Russians, the Turks would leave the Habsburg troops virtually unmolested.[23]

Despite Ostermann's reasoning, neither Ostein nor the Conference liked the plan at all. Instead of freeing the Austrians from the brunt of the Ottoman effort as the Russian minister had asserted, it seemed to expose them to all the fury the enemy could muster. Should the Russians march against Ochakov and the Crimea, the distances between them and the Austrians would be so great and communications so tenuous that mutual assistance would become impossible. Furthermore, the steppe the Russians had to cross offered such formidable logistical obstacles that a protracted siege could wreck the empress' army before it even encountered the Turks in a major battle. The result could be that the grand vizier, confident that the wasteland of the Ukraine and the Tartars

21 Ostein to emperor, February 2, 1737, in *ibid.*, Russland, II, 15.
22 Russian plan of joint operations, January 27/February 7, 1736/7, *ibid.*
23 Ostein to emperor, February 9, 1737, *ibid.*

would contain the Russians, would aim the bulk of his forces at the Habsburg frontier.[24]

These objections notwithstanding, the Conference accepted its ally's strategy, largely because it had no other choice. Barenklau and Ostein had no success in lobbying for a change in objectives, and Münnich's mid-February departure for the front with no alteration in orders signified that Ochakov would remain his primary target. In a token effort at least to secure communications between the armies, Vienna suggested that St. Petersburg dispatch a corps of irregular cavalry to northern Moldavia in order to make contact with the Austrian units in Transylvania.[25] Ostermann readily agreed and, apparently sensing his allies' uneasiness, reiterated his promise that, in the event the imperial forces met with difficulties, Münnich would lead his entire army to their relief.[26] In late March Ostein resignedly accepted the Russian operations plan on the emperor's behalf.[27]

This final agreement fittingly capped Ostermann's series of diplomatic successes over his maladroit allies. By first outlining the Russian campaign and then pronouncing it unchangeable, the Russian minister sidestepped Austrian attempts to use military cooperation to limit Russian conquests. In the Habsburg capital, the councillors still knew no more about the empress' objectives than they had in 1736 and now faced the unsettling prospect of fighting the Turks without aid. A Russian army before Ochakov was simply too far away to assist the Habsburg forces with either reinforcements

24 Bartenstein to emperor, March 7, 1737, in *ibid.*, Vorträge, 46.
25 *Ibid.*
26 Ostein to emperor, March 30, 1737, in *ibid.*, Russland, II, 15. Vienna knew that a great difference existed between Ostermann's promises and Münnich's deeds. Once he had joined his troops, the field marshal would do whatever pleased him, regardless of instructions from St. Petersburg.
27 *Ibid.* A published copy of this convention can be found in Martens, *Recueil des traités*, I, 80–84.

or a diversion, and none of Ostermann's assurances to the contrary could erase that fact.

All of the preparations with St. Petersburg now completed, if not entirely satisfactorily, Vienna turned its attention to the other courts of Europe in order to pacify potential enemies and recruit potential allies. For some time other western powers had speculated that the emperor intended to join the tsarina in her effort to pare the sultan's territory. As early as August, 1736, Horatio Walpole, brother of the celebrated British chief minister, noted:

> It is the prevailing opinion of the world, that the imperial court is disposed to act, not only on the score of friendship with Russia, but also with the flattering prospect of being able jointly with the Russ [sic] to make great advantages upon the Turks in their present weak and distracted condition, being in great confusion at home and hard-pressed by the Persians as well as the Muscovites abroad. The withdrawing of troops from Italy before matters are well-settled, the preparations in Hungary and on the side of Bosnia, with the setting out of the generals and other particulars, appear to be strong indications of some such resolution being privately taken in Vienna.[28]

In September Cardinal Fleury in Paris informed the Austrian ambassador that he had heard Vienna wished to annex Bosnia and Herzegovina, place the Hospodar of Moldavia under imperial protection, and ultimately eliminate the Ottoman Empire from Europe. The king of France could not tolerate such a disruption of the balance of power, warned the cardinal, and he hoped that the emperor understood that the weakening of Turkey would lead inevitably to an unwanted strengthening of Russia.[29]

28 Horatio Walpole to Rondeau, August 12/23, 1736, *Sbornik*, LXXX, 11.
29 Schmerling to emperor, September 23, 1736, in HHSA, SK, Russland, II, 132.

In November, to ease the conjecture and to justify his master's position, Bartenstein circulated to all courts a memorandum contending that the Porte's unprovoked attacks on Russia in 1733 and 1735 constituted acts of aggression against an Austrian ally—acts which Vienna could not possibly tolerate. Having committed these outrages and signed a peace with Persia, the Turks undoubtedly conspired to launch offensives first against Russia, then Austria, and finally the whole Christian world. Although anxious to maintain peace and appreciative of all European efforts to restrain the Porte, the secretary continued, the emperor must rush to the side of his ally, not only to protect a good friend but ultimately to defend himself.[30] Fully aware that few would accept these contentions as the real reasons for Austria's entering the struggle, Bartenstein nonetheless hoped that, in formal diplomacy, they would suffice to make the war "respectable in the eyes of the world." Such respectability could prove quite valuable when the time came to make peace, for the mediators of the era appreciated "legality and uprightness" when examining the demands of belligerents.[31]

Turning from general considerations to the attitudes of individual governments, the secretary believed that he needed to do nothing special to placate Austria's most recent enemies, France and Spain. In early December, 1736, Sinzendorf reported that his negotiations with the French regarding the final settlement of the Polish war were going so well that the emperor need not dread a renewal of hostilities in the west. Shortly thereafter came positive evidence of French goodwill when, in reply to a personal letter from Charles VI suggesting a closer relationship between France and Austria, Fleury of-

30 Emperor to all ministers, November 30, 1736, in *ibid.*, Türkei, 217.
31 Sinzendorf to Ostein, December 10, 1736, in *ibid.*, Russland, II, 132.

fered a rapprochement with Vienna "to strengthen peace throughout Europe"; and, almost as a token of his sincerity, ousted from his posts Germain-Louis Chauvelin, keeper of the king's seals and principal opponent of France's close association with the Habsburgs.[32] A final assurance of Paris's noninvolvement came from Constantinople, where the French ambassador, the Marquis Villeneuve, informed the grand vizier that his king would offer to mediate, but could not make a diversion, diplomatic or military, against Austria.[33] These manifestations of French benevolence naturally precluded Spanish bellicosity, for Spain would do nothing without its neighbor's approval and assistance.

Bartenstein knew it would be a mistake to rule out French and Spanish intervention entirely, however, for vocal factions demanding a renewal of hostilities against the Habsburgs existed in both countries. Their continued goodwill depended on the health of Fleury, already past his eighty-third birthday and suffering from periodic illness. So long as he determined French policy, Paris would never provide armed support to the Turks, but his death might permit a government unfriendly toward Austria to take power. Prayers for the cardinal's good health became a common feature of imperial court worship.[34]

32 Braubach, *Versailles und Wien*, 298. Chauvelin believed France's "natural allies" to be Spain and Bavaria and its "natural enemies" to be Austria, England, and Holland. Paul Vaucher, *Robert Walpole et la politique de Fleury, 1731–1742* (Paris, 1924), 186. Wilson points out that Chauvelin was removed because of opposition to Fleury's policies and not because of court intrigue. Wilson, *French Foreign Policy*, 274. See also Marquis d'Argenson, *Journal and Memoirs* (Boston, 1901), I, 102–105.

33 L'Abbé Laugier, *Histoire des négociations pour la paix conclue à Belgrade, le 18 septembre 1739* (Paris, 1768), I, 47–49. On January 26 Königsegg informed Talman that an envoy was leaving Paris for Constantinople with special orders to Villeneuve to encourage the Porte to make peace. Königsegg to Talman, January 26, 1737, in HHSA, SK, Türkei, 214.

34 Emperor to Ostein, November 23, 1736, in *ibid.*, Russland, II, 132.

Considering possible partners in the forthcoming struggle as well as possible enemies, Bartenstein hoped to persuade Vienna's old comrades in the Holy Alliance of 1684, Poland, Venice, the papacy, and the Diet of the Holy Roman Empire, to assist in the conflict. For the first two, however, prospects seemed dim. Still reconciling the rebellious elements in his own realm, Augustus III of Poland would hardly jeopardize his minimal popularity by participating in an unwanted war with the Turks.[35] Venice likewise would be reluctant to join because it still resented Austria's performance in the war of 1716–1718, when, although allied with Venice, the emperor signed a peace treaty without Venetian approval.[36] The papacy and the German princes, on the other hand, had no such grounds to reject a request for aid, and Bartenstein felt confident that they would respond favorably to his appeals for money and men.

In the summer and autumn of 1736, while the convolutions of the Russian negotiations and the European-wide diplomatic preparations occupied most of Vienna's time, one envoy who received scant attention was Baron Talman in Constantinople. His brief moment of glory had come in early July of that year when the emperor, as part of the strategy to extract a list of objectives from St. Petersburg, had granted him the title of ambassador and authorized him to renew Austria's offer to mediate a settlement between Russia and Turkey.[37] Not fully

35 The "pacification diet," in which all the Polish noblemen recognized Augustus as king, took place in June and July, 1736. Beyrich, "Kursachsen," 132.

36 Arneth, "Die Relationen der Botschafter Venedigs," 193.

37 *Resolutio Caesarea*, June 17, 1736, in HHSA, SK, Türkei, 213. The titles of foreign envoys were extremely important in diplomatic protocol. Were he not an ambassador, Talman would have found himself below the rank of the other envoys, should the Porte prefer the joint mediation of Austria and one or more other powers. Before becoming ambassador, Talman's official titles were *Resident*, November, 1728, to November, 1731, and *Internuntius*, November, 1731, to July, 1736. Friedrich Hausmann, *Repertorium der diplomatischen Vertreter aller Länder* (Zurich, 1950), II, 37.

appreciating the motives behind this maneuver, Talman accepted his assignment with enthusiasm and embarked on a vigorous campaign to win the sultan's favor. During the summer, however, he achieved little success, for the Porte quite understandably suspected Austrian motives, especially when Talman proved unable to provide a list of specific Russian demands or to explain the arrival of Austrian reinforcements along the Ottoman frontier.[38]

By August it appeared that Talman's time had been ill spent, because Vienna, now slowly moving toward a military commitment to Russia, ordered him to cease using the term "mediation" and employ instead the phrase "good offices to restore peace."[39] In diplomatic parlance this modification meant that, in future negotiations, Talman did not have to remain neutral but could support Russian demands; in effect it meant that Austria would soon drop its pose as innocent bystander and become an active participant in the war against Turkey.

At this juncture the baron disregarded these new orders and struck out on a course of his own. Certain that any alteration in terminology would expose his master's intention and prompt the Porte to strengthen its defenses along the Austrian border, Talman simply chose to ignore his instructions and allow "mediation" to stand.[40] To keep all alternative policies open and not to reveal to the Turks that the emperor had any ambition other than to restore peace became the ambassador's personal aim.[41]

38 Talman to Königsegg, July 24, 1736, in HHSA, SK, Türkei, 213.

39 *Resolutio Caesarea*, August 7, 1736, in *ibid.*, Russland, II, 217.

40 Talman to *Hofkriegsrat*, September 10, 1736, in *ibid.*, Türkei, 213.

41 Talman achieved remarkable success in disguising Austrian intentions, for in October the pasha of Vidin, in a letter to the governor of the Banat, inquired about the troop concentrations in Hungary, which, the pasha assumed, were directed "against the Russians." Emperor to Ostein, November 23, 1736, in *ibid.*, Russland, II, 132.

Talman's conduct in this matter, like Ostein's earlier, illustrates an essential element in Austria's actions in this particular war and in European diplomacy in general at that time: because of the absence of instant communication between the capital and its ambassadors abroad or military officers in the field, such officials possessed a great deal of liberty and responsibility in interpreting instructions from their superiors and the way in which these instructions related to conditions as they observed them. Frequently the success or failure of a policy depended upon the ability of a faraway minister to assess a situation accurately and act as he saw fit. For this reason much depended upon a government's selection of a man capable of carrying out its policies and, if necessary, of adjusting them to accord with unexpected circumstances.

Talman himself seemed an excellent minister. Son of an imperial resident in Constantinople and minister himself since 1728, he possessed a wealth of experience in and a keen understanding of Turkish politics, which perhaps persuaded him that by himself he could conduct a diplomatic strategy far more advantageous to the emperor than anything Vienna could concoct.[42] The ambassador overlooked only one consideration: he failed to see that his subtlety might cause a misunderstanding of Austrian motives in St. Petersburg and the other European capitals. If the other states believed his policy reflected that of Vienna, they would attribute to the emperor a sincere desire to avoid hostilities, a misconception that might alienate Russia and induce in the other governments a false confidence in the cause of peace. Consequently, instead of easing Austria's slide into war, Talman unwittingly complicated it.

The ambassador's behavior naturally caused concern in Vienna and prompted Königsegg to insist emphatically that

---

42 His father was Michael Talman, one of the plenipotentiaries at the negotiations leading to the Treaty of Passarowitz.

he drop "mediation" in favor of "good offices." By continuing to seek the position of mediator, admonished the war minister, Talman had disobeyed his superiors and had made relations with Russia more difficult.[43] But this reprimand hardly disturbed Talman, who responded that the emperor had never officially rescinded his offer to mediate, nor had the *Hofkriegsrat* canceled its orders for him to do all he could to hinder a break between Russia and Turkey. Until he received such revisions, he added, he would carry on his effort to bring about peace.[44] Coincidentally, while his answer was en route to Königsegg, Talman received notification from the Porte that the sultan would soon accept his services as arbiter and agree to a formal peace congress to resolve the Russo-Turkish quarrel.[45]

The ambassador's letter and the announcement of the Porte's intention to nominate him as mediator arrived in Vienna in late November, at a time when the Conference still awaited news from St. Petersburg concerning the status of the proposed convention with Russia. Fearful that Talman's appointment would jeopardize the allied negotiations and seriously hinder Bartenstein's European-wide efforts to brand Turkey the aggressor, the Habsburg ministers decided to convince the Ottomans that the emperor was far more interested in supporting Russia's side in the struggle than Talman might have led them to believe. To convey this message, Königsegg composed a personal letter to the grand vizier, stating that Turkish failure to comply with Russia's wishes

43 Königsegg to Talman, September 23, 1736, in *ibid.*, Türkei, 213.

44 Talman's excuses for his behavior had no foundation because the imperial resolution of August 7 and Königsegg's numerous letters specifically ordered him to cease using the term "mediation." Talman to *Hofkriegsrat*, October 20, 1736, *ibid.*

45 Grand Vizier Mohammed Pasha to Talman, *ibid.*, 212. The only date on this manuscript is that of November 8, 1736, recorded by the translator.

by the spring of 1737 would compel the emperor to abandon his desires for peace and resort to arms. No territorial ambitions inspired his master to reach this decision, the war minister assured the grand vizier, only the wish to aid an ally unjustly attacked.[46] In a note to Talman accompanying this letter, Königsegg told him to impress upon the Ottoman ministers the urgency of this warning, but not to threaten them or make them fearful of an immediate Austrian invasion.[47] Although anxious to discourage the Porte from accepting Talman's mediation, Vienna had no desire to incite the future enemy to undertake military preparations along the frontier.

Whatever its intention, this message had no effect on the Turks, who, in mid-December, invited Talman to join the grand vizier at his military headquarters at Babadag, 275 miles north of Constantinople. The summons meant that the Austrian ambassador had won the role of mediator and would be responsible for organizing a peace conference. On December 21, accompanied by a huge and sumptuous retinue and escorted for the first hour by a number of European envoys, he left his residence in Pera, a suburb of Constantinople, and set out for the Turkish war camp.[48] Three weeks later he arrived at Babadag and received his official appointment.

46 Königsegg to grand vizier, December 5, 1736, in *ibid.*, 214. This and subsequent letters from Königsegg to the grand vizier can be found in Johann Jacob Moser, *Der Belgradische Friedens-schluss zwischen ihro römisch-kayserl. Majestät und der ottomanische Pforte* (Jena, 1740).

47 Instructions to Talman, December 5, 1736, in HHSA, SK, Türkei, 214.

48 Talman reported that the escort included the old and new English envoys, the Venetian *bailo*, the Polish *internuncio*, and the Swedish minister. The French ambassador and his wife could not ride with the party but paid the appropriate respects before it left. The Dutch envoy was "too impolite to do either." Talman to *Hofkriegsrat*, January 2, 1737, *ibid.*

Having hoped that Königsegg's missive would forestall Turkish plans to accept Austrian mediation, Vienna was understandably mortified when the news of Talman's nomination arrived. To satisfy the requirements of diplomacy, the Conference knew that it had to sponsor a formal peace conference; but it also knew that the emperor could not simply adopt the posture of neutral mediator, because to do so would mean the renunciation of the military convention with Russia and would ultimately result in St. Petersburg's complete repudiation of the alliance.[49] To retain that alliance remained uppermost in Habsburg policy.

The only way out of this dilemma, it seemed to Bartenstein, was to manipulate the proceedings of the congress in order to provide the emperor with a convenient excuse for declaring war. That way the negotiations would be held, but Vienna would not have to renege on the promise to aid its ally. Toward that end the secretary wished Austria and Russia to formulate a series of "reasonable demands" (reasonable, that is, in the eyes of the other European powers), whose acceptance by the Turks would fulfill the allies' objectives while their rejection would justify Austria's entry into the war. But now Bartenstein had to determine what constituted reasonable demands. Luckily, as a matter of curiosity, in the autumn of 1736 he had inquired of the other European courts what terms they thought an honorable settlement might include. From the responses he drew up in January a projected peace treaty setting forth the following conditions: adjustment of the Russo-Turkish boundaries partly on the basis of *uti possidetis* (lands held by military conquest) and partly on the basis of the treaty of 1700, Russian retention of Azov and suzerainty over the Tartars of the Crimea and Kuban,

49 Bartenstein to emperor, February 24, 1737, in *ibid.*, Vorträge, 45.

and a renewal of the Peace of Passarowitz.[50] Having composed this proposal, the secretary undertook the uninviting chore of persuading the Russians to adopt it as their own, so that the allies could submit it as a joint program at the formal sessions.[51]

Bartenstein's appeals fell on deaf ears. Why should the empress reveal her demands now, inquired Ostermann upon receiving the secretary's terms, when direct negotiations between Russian and Turkish representatives looked so promising? It would be better to outline her wishes when the conferees met, he continued, for to do so earlier would only reduce her bargaining power.[52] With that reply vanished Vienna's hope that this particular tactic would serve to involve Austria honorably in the struggle.

While Bartenstein frantically sought a just pretext for the emperor to declare war, in Constantinople Talman busily conducted the preliminary negotiations for the forthcoming congress. By February all parties had agreed to meet and by March had elected their plenipotentiaries. Representing the Ottoman Empire would be the Reis Effendi Mustapha; the comptroller of finances Emini Mohammed Effendi; and the secretary of the feudal cavalry (Spahis), Mohammed Said Effendi, who had also served as special envoy and secretary of the legation in Moscow.[53] From Russia would come the aged Baron Peter Shafirov, senator, vice-chancellor, and prin-

50 Instructions to Talman, January 15, 1737, in *ibid.*, Türkei, 214. The treaty of 1700 gave Russia Azov and additional territory in the Ukraine, all of which returned to Ottoman possession by the treaty of 1711. For a published copy of the agreement of 1700, see Noradounghian, *Recueil d' actes internationaux*, 197–203. A common form of settlement in Turkish affairs, *uti possidetis* meant that each state received the land its army occupied at the time of the armistice.

51 Emperor to Ostein, January 23, 1737, in *ibid.*, Russland, II, 132.

52 Ostermann to Ostein, January 25/February 7, 1736/7, *ibid.*, 15.

53 Fawkener to Newcastle, January 8/19, 1736/7, *ibid.*

cipal negotiator at the Treaty of Pruth in 1711; Prince Artemus Volinsky, a veteran of Persian affairs; and, as head of
the team, Count Nepluyev, the former minister to Turkey.[54]
Talman, of course, would umpire, but, owing to his un-
popularity with Ostermann, would have the assistance of
Ostein as co-mediator.[55]

More difficult than appointing the delegates was selecting
a site. Although all assumed Poland would provide a convenient, neutral setting, the diplomats became enmeshed in
time-consuming discussions of locations in belligerent countries, which everyone knew would be unacceptable. The Russians began the process by suggesting their own city of Kiev,
"or any other place in the whole [Russian] Ukraine." [56] Somewhat irritated that St. Petersburg would nominate a Russian
city, the Turks offered instead the town of Soroki, which
they claimed lay in Poland, but which in reality rested on the
Turkish side of the Ottoman-Polish boundary.[57] Fully aware
of its exact position, Ostermann rejected Soroki and, as if
disgusted, put forth no alternative.[58]

This diplomatic fencing consumed most of the winter and
by early March the Turks, now regretting their obstinacy and
fearing that their army might suffer irreversible defeats once
the fighting resumed, expressed their anxiety to begin the
conference as soon as possible. Rather than suggest another
meeting place and await an answer, however, they notified
Talman, who in turn informed St. Petersburg, that their

54 Ostein to emperor, March 21, 1737, *ibid.* Ostein reported that
Ostermann chose Shafirov because of his experience and the other
two because they were his "creatures."
55 Bartenstein to emperor, January 20, 1737, in *ibid.*, Vorträge,
45.
56 Instructions to Talman, January 15, 1737, in *ibid.*, Türkei,
214.
57 Talman to Königsegg, February 14, 1737, *ibid.*
58 Ostermann to Ostein, March 9/20, 1737, in *ibid.*, Russland,
II, 15.

plenipotentiaries would set out for the Polish border, where, together with the Russian delegation and the Habsburg mediators, they could settle upon a city to serve as host.[59] Consequently in late March, Talman and the Turkish envoys left the grand vizier's camp for the Polish frontier. Depending upon the congress to furnish justifiable grounds for declaring war, the Habsburg advisers likewise had been anxious for the representatives to gather soon. But by mid-March they realized that their forces would clash with the Turks before the conference met and so turned to one last scheme to involve Austria honorably. They authorized König-segg to compose another letter to the grand vizier, this time announcing that if no settlement came forth by May 1—an impossible condition given the speed of eighteenth-century correspondence—the emperor must "act as Russia's loyal ally" and open hostilities.[60] Copies of this message went to the European capitals along with an explanation that Vienna had done what it could for peace and refused to tolerate any more delays. Although aware that the other powers would view this note merely as an excuse to launch an attack, the Conference hoped that they would also consider it diplomatically satisfactory for beginning a conflict. After the couriers carrying these copies had left Vienna, the councillors could at least console themselves that Europe could not formally accuse their master of outright aggression or of failing to give the Ottomans due warning.

Once again, as if destiny itself plotted against them, came news that their plans had gone awry. A few days before the May 1 deadline, Talman announced that he had chosen not to deliver Königsegg's letter on the grounds that the contents would so enrage the grand vizier that he would withdraw his

59 Talman to Ostein, February 23, 1737, *ibid.*
60 Königsegg to grand vizier, March 20, 1737, in *ibid.* Türkei, 215.

delegates from the peace congress. By this time determined to hold the conference whether or not Vienna approved, Talman would do nothing to endanger its meeting. If the negotiations continued concurrently with the fighting, the course of the war would undoubtedly affect the diplomatic maneuvering; and Talman believed that the summer's military developments would compel the Turkish representatives to accept a peace which would enhance the emperor's prestige and bring glory upon himself. Such a dream the ambassador would not permit Vienna to jeopardize.[61]

The Habsburg court received Talman's explanation with amazement. Why, the councillors wondered, in these troubled times did they have such difficulty keeping their subordinates from undermining their policies? To recall Talman would solve nothing, they decided, for the May 1 deadline had already passed, and he would still have to serve as formal mediator in the forthcoming talks. Nonetheless they could not allow him to escape without some form of reprimand.[62] Consequently the Conference instructed Königsegg to notify him—in the severest terms—that, by misrepresenting the emperor's intentions, he had lulled the Turks into a false sense of security, hurt Austrian trustworthiness in Europe, harmed relations with Russia, and ultimately marred Vienna's overall strategy. Despite his flagrant insubordination, Königsegg added, the ambassador must stay at his post, but the emperor expected complete obedience from him in the future.[63]

Notwithstanding the Conference's chagrin, Talman's independent efforts had little immediate impact on the course of events, for the Turks had suspected Habsburg intentions from

61 Talman to *Hofkriegsrat*, April 11, 1737, *ibid.* Vandal and Hammer claim that Talman told the *Hofkriegsrat* that the letter had been destroyed by mistake, but no evidence in Talman's own dispatches supports this hypothesis.
62 Konferenz Protokolle, April 28, 1737, in *ibid.*, Vorträge, 46.
63 Instructions to Talman, May 2, 1737, in *ibid.*, Türkei, 215.

the outset. Even while Vienna spoke of nothing but peace, the grand vizier had kept his army south of the Danube, ready to march instantly upon the imperial frontier. As for the consequences in western Europe, at the moment none of the powers appeared likely to use the Austrian ambassador's indiscretion to accuse the emperor of aggression. Nonetheless should any state decide at a later date to support the Ottoman Empire either diplomatically or militarily, Talman's failure to deliver the war minister's letter provided excellent grounds for arguing that Vienna had attacked the hapless Turks without due warning.

By May 1, 1737, it appeared that Habsburg diplomacy had met with total failure. Every effort to learn Russia's intentions and to convince Europe of the emperor's just motives had miscarried either because of the superior skill of Vienna's adversaries or the rebellious inclinations of its own representatives. Nonetheless the ultimate objective, the preservation of the Russian alliance, remained intact and its true value was again to be tested.

V

⚘ Disappointing Campaign and Fruitless Peace Congress

Throughout late 1736 and early 1737, as the councillors discussed and the diplomats negotiated Austria's entry into war, the *Hofkriegsrat* and the *Hofkammer* began the financial and military preparations to reinforce and re-equip the Habsburg troops on the Turkish border. By December, 1736, the army in southern Hungary, plagued by swamp fever and neglect, certainly needed refurbishing. Although officially numbering 58,000, the men had suffered such extensive illness that the total fit for service had fallen to only a fraction of that figure.[1] In fact conditions had deteriorated to the point that in October the *Hofkriegsrat* had been compelled to dissolve one of the four battalions in each regiment in order to bring the remaining three up to strength.[2] With the outbreak of hostilities now approaching, the *Hofkriegsrat* had to replace these losses, transfer additional units to the camps, and organize logistical support for a large field army.

The initial task in readying the forces belonged not to the

1 Brown, "Türkenkrieg," 1737, Appendix G.
2 Konferenz Protokolle, January 18, 1737, in HHSA, SK, Vorträge, 45.

Hofkriegsrat, but to the *Hofkammer*, the office in charge of procuring funds to finance recruitment and supply. To raise the 5,000,000 *gulden* necessary for one year's campaign, the *Hofkammer* decided to ask first the Estates of the emperor's crownlands to contribute as much as possible to this sum. At first fearful that the Estates would sacrifice no more after the disappointments of the War of the Polish Succession, the finance officials found, to their surprise, that the people greeted the forthcoming struggle with enthusiasm. Apparently confident that their army could easily defeat the Turks, they looked upon the conflict as an opportunity for their troops to win land, booty, and glory for the emperor. One contemporary reported "As I was in Vienna at this time . . . , I heard it said that the Grand Vizier, not wanting to make war and well aware of the poor state of the Turkish army in comparison to that of the Emperor, wanted to avoid a clash if he could and that the sweetness which appeared in his letter was only a sign of his reluctance [to fight]. The tone of these discourses flattered the populace and increased the hope of great conquest." [3]

Encouraged by the prospect of success, the crownlands promised more than enough for one campaign. In addition to the normal contribution which reached 8,000,000 *gulden*, Silesia pledged 3,500,000 *gulden* as credit for a loan in Holland, the Hungarian nobility donated 200,000, and the Tyrolean salt works provided collateral for an advance of 3,000,000 *gulden* from the Swiss cantons. Adding to these sources, the emperor proclaimed a "Turkish tax," the tax traditionally issued during Turkish wars. [4]

From foreign sources the *Hofkammer* received substantial funds as well. The pope levied a five-year tithe on Austrian

3 La Lande, *Histoire de l'empereur Charles VI*, IV, 553.
4 Proclamation of the Turkish tax, April 7, 1737, in HHSA, SK, Türkei, 215.

church property to raise 1,000,000 *gulden* per year and contributed another 2,850,000 from the Vatican treasury. From the Diet of the Holy Roman Empire, Vienna secured an additional 3,000,000 *gulden*, and Saxony and Wolfenbüttel offered military contingents to help with the fighting.[5]

When these monies came in, they passed to the *Hofkriegsrat* for use in procuring men, animals, equipment, and provisions. The office ordered the recruitment of 20,000 men, the purchase of 5,000 cavalry mounts, and the manufacture of various numbers of fortress cannon, fieldpieces, mortars, river warships, and transport vessels. To provision and service this grand array, the *Hofkriegsrat* requisitioned manifold supplies and commissioned the necessary carts and oxen to carry them to appointed magazines.[6] Soon troops and military paraphernalia bound for Hungary began to pass daily through Vienna.

With preparations for war progressing, Charles and his advisers tackled the task of selecting a commander in chief. From 1703 to 1736, there had been no need for such a decision because Prince Eugene, standing far above the other imperial officers in talent, experience, and prestige, had always assumed the supreme command. In 1737, however, the great genius lay dead and someone new had to take his place.

At this time choosing a leader from among the remaining officers proved quite difficult because two factions had emerged to compete for control of the military apparatus after Eugene's death; to appoint a commander from one naturally meant incurring the resentment of the other. Of these two groups, the stronger, labeled the Protestant triumvirate, consisted of Field Marshal Frederic Henry Seckendorf, General

5 Mensi, *Finanzen*, 662.
6 Brown, "Türkenkrieg," 1737, Appendix CC. This appendix lists in detail all the needs of supplies, munitions, and so forth, and where all of this material is to be found. Major stores were located in Vienna, Budapest, and Belgrade.

Schmettau, and Prince Sachsen-Hildburghausen.[7] Within this clique, the youngest, Hildburghausen, held the greatest favor with the emperor. In addition to his superior knowledge and experience in Balkan affairs, he possessed youth, dash, vigor, and self-assurance that won for him special attention from both Charles VI and his wife.[8] Although scorned by Prince Eugene as a "loser of battles" and a "general of retreat," Hildburghausen became the great hope of Charles VI and Bartenstein in military affairs.[9]

Opposed to the Protestant triumvirate stood the so-called Catholic party, led by Count John Palffy and Count Louis Khevenhüller and "innocently" supported by the emperor's son-in-law, Francis Stephen of Lorraine. Although identified by religion, this group had no theological prejudice against the other, but resented primarily the youthful Hildburghausen, who had more influence with the emperor than did the senior officers.[10] To reduce the prince's prominence constituted the major objective of the Catholic party's intrigue.

In the duel for the coveted assignment of commander in chief, the Protestant triumvirate emerged triumphant, for in April, 1737, Charles appointed Seckendorf to the post. Sixty-three years old, Seckendorf appeared "a small man, devoid of either grace or charm, but intelligent, tough, and endowed with an immense capacity for work." [11] First noticed by Prince Eugene in the War of the Spanish Succession, during which he served under the flags of the Netherlands, the German Empire, and Prussia, he had entered the Habsburg service in

---

7 Schmettau, *Mémoires secrets*, 20–21. Seckendorf and Schmettau were Protestants; Hildburghausen was a convert to Roman Catholicism.
8 Braubach, "Eine Satire auf den Wiener Hof," 61–62.
9 Hrazky, "Johann Christoph Bartenstein," 238.
10 Schmettau, *Mémoires secrets*, 18.
11 Lavender Cassels, *The Struggle for the Ottoman Empire, 1717–1740* (London, 1966), 122.

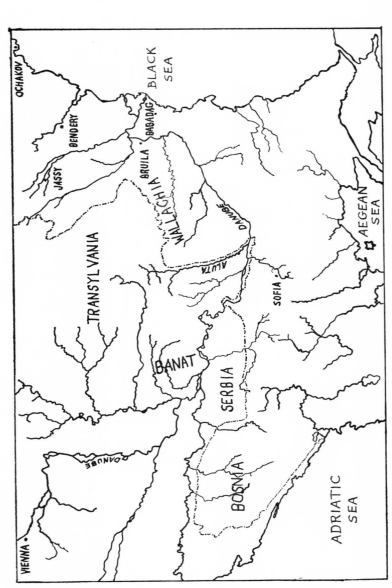

Southeastern Europe, 1737–1739

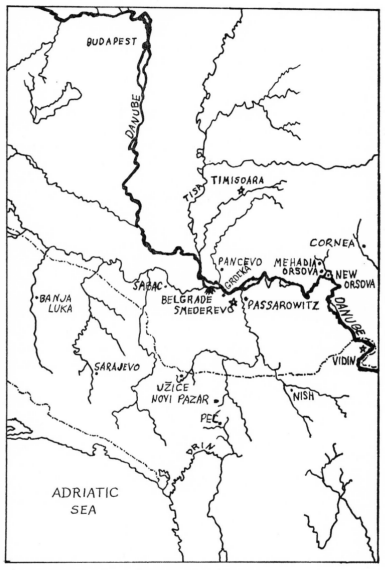

Scene of Austrian Campaigns, 1737–1739

1717 and became "one of the best and most effective generals in the imperial army."[12] An accomplished diplomat as well as an able officer, the field marshal, while minister in Berlin in the 1720s, had "practically become" the most important adviser to the Prussian king, Frederick William I, on questions of foreign policy.[13]

But the Protestant victory had certain limitations. To conciliate the disgruntled Catholic party, Charles ordered the new commander in chief to follow strictly the operations plan composed by the *Hofkriegsrat* and to consult his subordinates on all problems of strategy. Aware that this restriction on his authority would irritate Seckendorf, the emperor also sent his son-in-law as a "volunteer" to learn the art of war, but more importantly to make certain that no factionalism broke out among the senior officers that could be detrimental to the Austrian war effort.[14] Despite these efforts at compromise, Seckendorf deeply resented this departure from the common practice of allowing the commanding officer virtually unrestricted authority in the field and, as an expression of his resentment, frequently ignored the advice of his staff. This behavior increased animosity among the senior officers, and, before long, discontent permeated headquarters from top to bottom.

On May 30, 1737, the high-ranking officers of the Habs-

12 Arneth, *Prinz Eugen*, III, 18–19, 440.
13 *Ibid.*, 200–202. Frederick William remained a good friend of Seckendorf and, upon hearing of his disgrace in October, 1737, commented: "Had Seckendorf done anything criminal against the Emperor and the House of Austria, I would bet my head that he did not do it. That is what happens when one serves an imbecilic master." Frederick William I to Leopold zu Anhalt-Dessau, November 15, 1737, Friedrich Wilhelm I, *Die Briefe Friedrich Wilhelms I an den Fürsten Leopold zu Anhalt-Dessau, 1704–1740* (Berlin, 1905), 618–19.
14 Brown, "Türkenkrieg," 1737, Appendices KK, LL. Charles instructed Francis Stephen to watch particularly for ill feeling between Seckendorf and Khevenhüller.

burg army left Vienna for their posts in southern Hungary. They hoped to march immediately against a major Turkish force near Vidin, inflict a crushing defeat upon it, and, in conjunction with two auxiliary corps deployed in Bosnia and Wallachia, occupy as much Ottoman territory as possible.[15] Upon arriving at the military camps, however, they found their troops in no condition to attack. Not only did the army lack wagons, pontoon bridges, hospital facilities, and transport boats, but many of the regiments had not yet arrived at their muster points. Adding to the confusion, officials from the *Hofhammer* and the *Hofkriegsrat* had engaged in disputes over which body had responsibility for the distribution of funds and thus failed to provide the regimental commanders with money to pay their men.[16] Owing to this administrative disorder, Seckendorf reported to Vienna that he needed a month to prepare his forces and could not open hostilities until at least early July.[17]

Taking advantage of this unwanted delay, the Conference gathered on June 14 to review for the last time the decision to go to war. Even at this late date some doubt remained, chiefly in the mind of Count Königsegg. Citing reports from Hungary that the Danubian water level had risen high enough to hinder operations against Vidin and increase the danger of malaria spreading among the men, the president of the *Hofkriegsrat* argued that the soldiers should remain in camp that season and wait until next year to launch the attack. Besides, he continued, the only reason for mounting this campaign was to help the Russians, and, because no word had

15 *Ibid.*, 1737, p. 110.
16 *Ibid.*, 118–35. These pages contain 2 reports from Seckendorf concerning the condition of the army in June, 1737. Somewhat contrary to these descriptions, Lorraine wrote that the army was in better condition than even Vienna had hoped. Arneth, *Geschichte Maria Theresia's*, I, 37.
17 Brown, "Türkenkrieg," 1737, p. 145.

arrived that they themselves had engaged the enemy, why not postpone operations indefinitely?

Despite Königsegg's objections, the Conference decided in favor of immediate war, largely because the diplomatic groundwork had already been laid; and, as Count Starhemberg noted, malaria would more likely grip the men if they remained in the unsanitary conditions of their camps than if they marched into the field.[18] Essentially, all the preparations had been completed and it was simply too late to stop now.

On July 14 a great procession, including representatives from the religious orders, tribunals, holy and secular guilds, hospitals, and schools, imperial ministers, court aristocrats, and the emperor himself, wound its way from the *Hofburg* to St. Stephen's Cathedral to announce to the city of Vienna the outbreak of hostilities. After gathering before the main doors of the cathedral, the paraders and onlookers heard the formal declaration of war and an edict proclaiming that, at the sound of church bells ringing every morning at 7:00, each individual should drop his work, fall on his knees, and pray for the blessing of the Almighty upon the arms of the emperor.[19] On the same day, some four hundred miles to the southeast, an imperial officer presented the same declaration of war to the pasha of Nish. Expressing surprise the pasha asked for a ten-day respite to procure orders from Constantinople concerning his course of action; but, upon receiving the request, Seckendorf denied it, and shortly thereafter the Austrian army crossed into Turkish land.[20]

Before the campaign had even begun, however, the first

18 Konferenz Protokolle, June 14, 1737, and Bartenstein to emperor, June 16, 1737, in HHSA, SK, Vorträge, 46.
19 La Lande, *Histoire de l'empereur Charles VI*, II, 563–64. Sinzendorf suggested the procession because the war had been kept "very quiet." Sinzendorf to Emperor, July 6, 1737, in HHSA, SK, Vorträge, 47.
20 Brown "Türkenkrieg," 1737, pp. 172–80.

hint of future adversity appeared. Without consulting his officers or seeking Vienna's approval, Seckendorf in late June announced that, because of heavy flooding along the Danube, he would besiege Nish rather than Vidin.[21] Although jolted by this unauthorized change of plans and concerned that the proper provisions could not be transferred quickly enough to supply the men, the Conference decided not to override the commander in chief, largely because his operations to march his army to Nish would already be under way before such orders reached him. Nonetheless conjecture spread that the emperor's difficulty with his subordinates had by no means come to an end.[22]

At first this deviation from the original strategy seemed a stroke of good fortune, for, as soon as the Austrian army appeared before Nish, the pasha of the fortress surrendered, and, except for an inexpensive guarantee of safe conduct to the nearest Turkish encampment for the pasha and his men, the victory had cost nothing.[23] Apparently wishing to savor this success, Seckendorf, instead of advancing quickly on Vidin before the grand vizier could march his field army to Wallachia, quartered his troops in and around Nish and dispatched only a corps to Vidin to serve as an observation force.[24]

Following the commander in chief's success, the only other Austrian military operation of note to occur in July consisted of an expedition into Bosnia to encourage the Orthodox Serbian patriarch of Peć to declare his allegiance and that of his flock to the emperor.[25] By no means an original device in

21 *Ibid.*, 142–45, 346–49.
22 Angeli, "Krieg mit der Pforte," 287.
23 Brown, "Türkenkrieg," 1737, pp. 187–91. For terms of the capitulation, see Appendix SS.
24 *Ibid.*, 201, 203–204.
25 On March 8, 1737, a representative from the patriarch of Peć told the Habsburg commander at Belgrade that the patriarch would place himself and his followers under imperial protection if war erupted between Austria and Turkey. Johann Langer, "Nord-Alba-

Viennese strategy, since 1683 such appeals to the Serbs to overthrow their Moslem overlords had gone out each time the emperor had declared war on the sultan. Sometimes such entreaties carried substantial weight; in 1688, for example, the Serbs exerted such efforts on behalf of the Austrians that, when the Habsburg troops fell back in the face of an Ottoman counter-thrust, 30,000 Serbs and their spiritual chieftains fled into imperial territory to escape Turkish reprisals.[26]

Each time the pleas for revolt reached the Serbs from Vienna, the Serbian religious officials—who doubled as the political and military leaders—requested some form of reward and a modicum of support, and 1737 proved no exception. On this particular occasion, as his payment, the patriarch of Peć received the appointment of Orthodox Metropolitan of Belgrade and, as armed assistance, an expeditionary force of a hussar regiment and 1,000 mounted irregulars under the command of Colonel Robert Lentulus.[27] Setting out from the Austrian camp in mid-July, Lentulus and his men reached their objective, the village of Novi Pazar, with little trouble and there met the patriarch and a small body of Serbian volunteers.[28]

Not long after his arrival, however, Lentulus encountered problems that eventually rendered his position at Novi Pazar untenable. First the hussars left his command to quell a robber plague in Hungary, and then 500 replacements, sent from Seckendorf to compensate for the loss of the hussars, stumbled into a Turkish ambush on the way and were destroyed.[29]

---

niens und der Herzegovina Unterwerfungs-Anerbieten an Österreich, 1737–1739," *Archiv für österreichische Geschichte*, LXII (1881), 247.

26 See Wayne S. Vucinich, "The Serbs in Austria-Hungary," *Austrian History Yearbook*, III (1967), Pt. 2, p. 11.

27 Émile Picot, *Les Serbes de Hongrie* (Paris, 1873), 111.

28 Brown, "Türkenkrieg," 1737, p. 202.

29 *Ibid.*, 203–208.

Shortly thereafter, a larger force of 1,000 horse and 1,000 foot, also dispatched by Seckendorf, ran out of supplies en route to Novi Pazar and, unable to procure adequate provisions from the surrounding countryside, turned about and went back to Nish.[30] By late August, having received no reinforcements and now facing a Turkish offensive, Lentulus withdrew from Novi Pazar and, after conducting the patriarch and 2,000 of his followers to Belgrade, rejoined the main army.[31]

This expedition marked the only serious Austrian effort to foment a rising among the Balkan Christians during this war.[32] Owing to the limited response among the Serbs in the Novi Pazar area—Lentulus had no success finding volunteers and virtually none securing provisions—Vienna concluded that this time the Balkan Christians were uninterested in helping their co-religionists fight the Ottomans. Perhaps also these people appreciated the potential danger in their supporting the Austrians, for, should the Habsburg army fail to conquer their territory, they would either have to flee their homes for Austrian land or suffer severe retribution at the hands of the Turks. In mid-August, 1737, Seckendorf himself reported that the Christian nations would not rise unless the Habsburg forces actually occupied their land, an impossible condition, the commander added, because it would put too heavy a strain on the Austrian supply system.[33] In the next two years

30 *Ibid.*, 209.
31 *Ibid.*, 222.
32 In 1738 the *Hofkriegsrat* authorized General de la Cerda de Villa Longa to raise soldiers from the Serbs who had fled to the Habsburg lands. The general had visions of himself "at the head of 80,000 soldiers and peasants marching on Constantinople. He even imagined the coronation of Francis Stephen, the Emperor's son-in-law, in Hagia Sophia." Instead of 80,000, he recruited only a few hundred, and these proved unmanageable. Langer, "Nord-Albaniens," 250–51, 269–75.
33 Brown, "Türkenkrieg," 1737, p. 227.

of struggle, the emperor did issue periodic manifestos calling upon the Serbs to revolt, but they seemed mere formalities rather than serious efforts to inspire rebellion.[34]

While the armies maneuvered in the theaters of war, the delegates to the almost-forgotten peace congress assembled at the small Ukrainian city of Nemirov, the site finally chosen as suitable for the negotiations. Resting on the left bank of the Bug River, about two days ride from the Ottoman border and four days from the Russian, Nemirov represented the major Polish military base in the southern Ukraine. Passing through this city in December, 1737, John Bell, an Englishman in the employ of the Russian foreign ministry, described it as "pretty large and populous, well-fortified, and garrisoned. The country about Nemiroff [sic] is very pleasant and fruitful, having many orchards in the neighborhood, which produce the largest apples and pears that I have ever seen anywhere." [35] Nemirov belonged to Count Nicholas Potocki, grand general of Poland and, ironically, a member of the most outspokenly anti-Russian family in the kingdom.[36]

By the end of May, Talman and the Turks had arrived at this community, but the Russians, hoping to stall the opening of the congress in order to allow their armies to overrun as much Ottoman land as possible, failed to appear until early

34 According to Zinkeisen, the Austrians also conducted talks with the archbishop of Ochrid, who demanded, as payment for his cooperation, imperial protection, religious freedom for himself and his followers, elevation of himself to spiritual and temporal head of Bosnia, Serbia, and Albania, and a seat and vote in the Diet of the Holy Roman Empire. Zinkeisen, *Geschichte des osmanischen Reiches*, V, 720. In the autumn of 1737, two individuals from Herzegovina contacted the Austrian army headquarters and offered 30,000 men to help rout the Turks. Both men went to Vienna, where they negotiated with the *Hofkriegsrat* for two years, but with no results. Langer, "Nord-Albaniens," 253.

35 John Bell, *Travels from St. Petersburg in Russia to various Parts of Asia* (Edinburgh, 1806), 582.

36 Manstein, *Contemporary Memoirs*, 184.

July.[37] Even then the Russians managed to prolong the preliminary talks concerning procedure and protocol, so that the first formal session did not take place until August 16.[38]

When the meetings finally began, they took place in a large tent with two small tents at either end for the delegations to gather. Inside the large tent stood two tables pushed against each other, the Turks sitting face-to-face with the Russians and Austrians at the other. Entering the tent at precisely 10:00 A.M., the plenipotentiaries seated themselves simultaneously, the Turks on a long sofa and the Russians and Austrians on easy chairs, all at the same height. On the allied side, the Austrian representatives sat on the right because, as official mediators—although by then active belligerents—they assumed the more honorable position.[39] On the first day the envoys exchanged credentials, and Ostein opened the congress with a long, tedious speech in Latin, extolling the virtues of peace and harmony among states.[40]

On August 19, at the third session of the conference, the moment came for which the Austrians had waited since 1735: the Russians revealed their war aims. The scope of these aims confirmed Vienna's fears, for, based on the principle of *uti possidetis*, they included annexation of the Crimea and Kuban, free trade for Russian merchants in the Ottoman Empire, and—most important for Habsburg interests—estab-

37 Talman dispatched a letter dated May 27, 1737 from Soroki, indicating that he and his Turkish companions had encamped within easy reach of Nemirov. Talman to *Hofkriegsrat*, May 27, 1737, in HHSA, SK, Türkei, 215. Ostein left St. Petersburg on June 14 and arrived at Nemirov on or a few days before July 10. *Privat Protokolle* of Nemirov, in *ibid.*, Kreigsakten, 324.

38 *Privat Protokolle* of Nemirov, *ibid.*

39 Rondeau to Harrington, August 13/24, 1737, *Sbornik*, LXXX, 190. Although the position of the Austrians both as belligerents and mediators appeared odd indeed, the Turks, apparently at this time still hoping to reach an early settlement, raised no objections.

40 *Privat Protokolle* of Nemirov, 324.

lishment of Moldavia and Wallachia as independent Orthodox principalities under Russian protection.[41]

As everyone attending the conference understood, the strength of demands presented by each side would be judged on the basis of reports from the battlefields. News of victory would prompt a belligerent to put forth its widest claims; news of defeat might cause it to ask for nothing at all. When the empress' delegates exposed their extensive requests, it seemed that they had every good reason to do so: on July 13 the Russian army had stormed the mighty fortress of Ochakov and inflicted a resounding defeat upon the enemy. The success had seemed most convincing, for the messengers related that, on the second day of the siege, the Turks's main powder magazine had exploded, destroying most of the town and fortifications, after which the Russians poured into the now defenseless city and massacred 17,000 of the 20,000 garrison troops.[42] With Ochakov in their hands, the Russians could advance into Moldavia with relative ease.

This formal description, however, had told only part of the story, and, by the second week of August, the plenipotentiaries at Nemirov discovered that the Russian victory was not as complete as the first reports portrayed. From the Austrian attaché to Russian headquarters, Colonel Barenklau, they learned that, instead of overwhelming the enemy by superior might, the empress' army had captured the fortress by sheer good fortune—the explosion of the powder magazine. They were also told that the Russians had suffered such severe losses, that at one point Count Münnich had thrown down his sword and proclaimed all was lost. After offering this descrip-

41 *Ibid.*
42 Manstein, *Contemporary Memoirs*, 159. See also Burchard Christoph von Münnich, "Tagebuch über den ersten Feldzug in den Jahren 1735–1739 geführten russisch-türkischen Krieges," in Ernst Hermann (ed.), *Beiträge zur Geschichte des russischen Reiches* (Leipzig, 1843), 117–243.

tion of the encounter, Barenklau went on to suggest that, despite the conquest, casualties precluded any more fighting this year; and, instead of moving southward, the field marshal would withdraw from Ochakov and return his battered forces to the Ukraine.[43]

In light of the colonel's report, not only the Turkish but the Austrian delegates as well rejected the idea that Russian success had made the demands acceptable. In fact the first to reply to the presentation of these articles was Ostein, who launched a tirade condemning them as totally absurd. Each land St. Petersburg claimed by right of conquest, he raged, had either never been occupied or would shortly be evacuated by the empress' troops, and he could not see how his allies dared even suggest such all-encompassing acquisitions when their military performance had fallen so far short of expectations.[44] After Ostein's temper subsided, the Reis Effendi announced that he could never accept the Russian terms; the surrender of Moldavia and Wallachia did not merit discussion, and, as for the Crimea, the sultan would rather lose Constantinople itself than the country of his loyal Tartars. Concluding by reminding the Russian envoys that their requests in no way corresponded to their announced *casus belli*, the suppression of Tartar aggression, the Reis Effendi moved the termination of the stormy session and it accordingly adjourned.[45]

Notwithstanding Ostein's dramatic expression of surprise,

43 Talman and Ostein to *Hofkriegsrat*, August 4 and 5, 1737, in HHSA, SK, Türkei, 216. In his report Barenklau noted that the Russian troops showed great courage, "but as to the generals, they were all of them, without exception, only fit at the most to be captains of grenadiers." The Russian delegates sent a copy of this letter to Ostermann, who passed it to Münnich. After reading it, the field marshal reproached Barenklau personally and demanded his recall. Vienna dutifully complied and Barenklau left Russia at the end of 1737. Manstein, *Contemporary Memoirs*, 195–96.

44 *Privat Protokolle* of Nemirov, 324.

45 Ostein and Talman to emperor, August 20, 1737, HHSA, SK, Türkei, 216.

the Austrians had expected the Russian demands, fearing from the beginning that their allies would try to seize possession of Moldavia and Wallachia. But the timing, more than the scope, of the claims startled them. Had the storming of Ochakov been indeed an unqualified success or had the Russian delegates not known of Barenklau's report—which they had even read—then the Habsburg representatives could have at least appreciated such all-inclusive articles. However, to bring them forth as the Russian armies retreated after minimal success seemed not only ludicrous, but damaging to the prospects of reaching an acceptable settlement at the congress.[46]

Despite the Austrians' inability to understand the Russians' timing, they had little opportunity to speculate because on August 22 they had to lay their own demands before the other delegates. As mentioned earlier, the Conference had given relatively little thought to war aims, although it had generally conceded that the emperor should receive something for his pains and should have some terms to present at the peace negotiations. In the spring of 1737 Bartenstein suggested that the Conference consider some definite claims, but quickly added that, should the army suffer any serious setback, the emperor must conclude an immediate settlement without annexations.[47] Not until the end of July, after hearing of Seckendorf's conquest of Nish, did the Conference compose a formal set of terms for the peace congress.[48] Assuming that the commander in chief would march from Nish to Vidin while auxiliary corps advanced deep into Ottoman territory to the north and south, it decided to claim all of Bosnia and western Wallachia as its indemnity for having to fight. Whether or

46 *Ibid.*
47 Bartenstein to emperor, March 7, 1737, in *ibid.*, Vorträge, 46.
48 On July 9 the Conference met to consider Austria's *desideria pacis* but postponed any decision until it saw "how God would crown the Emperor's arms." Konferenz Protokolle, July 9, 1737, *ibid.*, 47.

not to ask for Vidin remained the only problem, but the Conference resolved it simply by instructing Talman and Ostein to base their claims upon the military situation. If, by the time they offered their articles to the congress, Seckendorf had conquered the fortress, they should demand its cession; if not, they should leave it to the sultan. When the Austrian representatives presented these points on August 22, Vidin still remained in Turkish hands, thus it did not constitute part of the Emperor's proposals.[49]

In noticeable contrast to the airing of the Russian requests, the presentation of the Habsburg terms barely elicited a reaction at the congress.[50] Instead of commenting on the Austrian proposals, the Reis Effendi announced that, seeing the discussion had now encompassed affairs outside his authority, he would have to ask permission of the other delegates to send a messenger to the grand vizier for additional instructions. To the Austrians, this request obviously meant that the Turks sensed a turnabout in military fortunes, and, in the time required for the courier to reach the official and return, hoped that their forces could regain the offensive. Although intensely disliking this delay, the allied plenipotentiaries had no choice but to give their approval, for, in diplomatic practice, to refuse would terminate the congress and place the onus for ending it squarely upon themselves. Estimating that six weeks would pass before the courier returned, the delegates settled down to wait.[51]

In that six weeks, it became increasingly evident that the military tide had indeed turned, for not only was Münnich departing for the Ukraine, as Barenklau had guessed he

49 Emperor to Talman, August 1, 1737, in *ibid.*, Türkei, 216.
50 *Privat Protokolle* of Nemirov, 324.
51 Talman to *Hofkriegsrat*, September 6, 1737, HHSA, SK, Türkei, 216. Ostein and Talman insisted that the grand vizier's instructions arrive by October 15, or they would consider the conference dissolved because of Turkish bad faith.

would, but the Austrian offensive had dissolved into purposeless activity. Instead of moving on to Vidin after a short rest, Seckendorf had kept his main force outside Nish and sent only a corps under Count Khevenhüller to observe Vidin and to prevent Turkish reinforcements and supplies from reaching it. Believing his force too weak for this assignment, however, Khevenhüller merely occupied the heights overlooking the objective and refused to undertake any offensive action until more men reached him from the commander in chief. In late August, Seckendorf himself gathered with his senior officers to discuss the situation; because of supply problems, illness, and the possible appearance of a Turkish relief force, the majority advised against initiating a siege.[52] Unfortunately no action at all was taken, and the Turks managed to advance additional troops and supplies to the fortress, which soon became sufficiently strong to weather a long and arduous siege.[53]

While Khevenhüller and Seckendorf dallied in Serbia, a major encounter took place in Bosnia, where auxiliary units under Hildburghausen, in the process of investing the Turkish fortress of Banja Luka, engaged a strong Turkish relief army sent to raise the siege. Caught by surprise and with his forces divided in half by the Vrbas River, the prince could not unify his soldiers into a single body to repulse the attack. Consequently, although still in possession of one bank at the end of the battle, the Austrians suffered such severe casualties (66 officers and 922 men killed and wounded) that they had to retire from Banja Luka to positions behind the Sava River.[54]

The clash at Banja Luka and Hildburghausen's retreat at last prompted Seckendorf to take action, although of the wrong kind. Believing that this defeat opened most of Croatia to Turkish penetration, the commander in chief resolved to

52 Brown, "Türkenkrieg," 1737, pp. 263–67.
53 Zinkeisen, *Geschichte des osmanischen Reiches*, V, 723.
54 Angeli, "Krieg mit der Pforte," 298–306.

march his principal force back into Bosnia, avenge the prince's losses, secure Bosnia and the Croatian border, and then return to Vidin to take up the long-awaited siege.[55] Actually such a maneuver was unnecessary, for Hildburghausen needed no help. As the prince himself advised the field marshal, he knew from informants that only 30,000 Turks, the largest body being 4,000, occupied Bosnia; and, despite his setback, he planned to return soon, confident of his ability to make good his losses and win the province for the emperor.

Even more important than providing aid to someone who did not need it, however, the commander in chief's withdrawal of the main army to Bosnia left only Khevenhüller's corps, the garrison at Nish, and scattered forces in Wallachia to defend the imperial positions in the east against a Turkish counteroffensive.[56] Unfortunately that counteroffensive would not be long in coming, for in early September the grand vizier, apparently assured that the Russian threat had vanished, was moving his troops westward in preparation for an assault on the Habsburg front in Serbia.

Even before the Turks launched their final thrust against the Austrians, the news of Hildburghausen's defeat, Seckendorf's expedition to Bosnia, and Münnich's departure for winter quarters had a noticeable impact on the atmosphere of relations at Nemirov. As they saw their military advantages slowly disappear, the Russian and Austrian representatives became increasingly hostile toward one another. Accusing each other's armies of having failed to bring about the decisive

55 Brown, "Türkenkrieg," 1737, pp. 329. A war council composed of Seckendorf, Khevenhüller, Count Oliver Wallis, the duke of Lorraine, and the Saxon general Sulkowsky authorized this decision on August 29, 1737.

56 Schmettau, *Mémoires secrets*, 53, 58, 59. Although Schmettau claims that the Conference ordered Seckendorf to go to Bosnia because the courtiers in Vienna feared Turkish raids on their estates in Carinthia and Carniola, no evidence of such an order exists in the Conference protocols or Brown's manuscript.

victories expected of them, the allied plenipotentiaries railed against each other's demands, each blaming the other for obstructing the path to a satisfactory settlement.[57] Intense bitterness developed especially between Ostein and the chief Russian negotiator Nepluyev, the former confessing that he truly loathed the latter.[58]

The Austrian plenipotentiaries and their Ottoman and Russian counterparts continued their waiting until mid-October, when the Turks at last announced the arrival of their messenger and called for a reconvening of the congress. At this point Ostein and Talman expected a complete rejection of all demands but still hoped the Turks would consent to continue the congress in order to work out a compromise later in the autumn.[59] These hopes suffered a bitter blow, for at the formal session held on October 15, the Turks not only repudiated the Russian and Austrian claims, but presented a list of their own, which included the return of Ochakov to the Ottoman Empire and the removal of the Russian-supported Cossacks from the Ukraine. Quite naturally the Russian envoys repudiated these terms outright, but, quite unexpectedly, the Turks responded by stalking out of the meeting. The next day the Ottoman delegation left Nemirov for Constantinople; the Austrians and Russians had no choice but to pack their belongings and depart as well.[60]

Ironically, one day after the congress broke up, the Austrian army suffered the final indignity of its inept campaign. On October 11 a Turkish cavalry squadron appeared before the gates of Nish to announce the arrival of an army of 80,000

---

57 Talman and Ostein to *Hofkriegsrat*, September 17 and 27, 1737, in HHSA, SK, Russland, II, 134.

58 Ostein to Sinzendorf, September 17, 1737, in *ibid.*, Türkei, 216.

59 *Privat Protokolle* of Nemirov, 324.

60 Talman and Ostein to *Hofkriegsrat*, October 17, 1737, HHSA, SK, Türkei, 217. Talman wrote that the Turkish servants had already departed with tents and baggage before the decisive session of October 15.

men, personally commanded by Ahmed Kiuprili, bearer of one of the most illustrious names in Ottoman history.[61] Inside the fortress the garrison commander, General Doxat de Morez, calculated that, although he had provisions to last for six weeks, he had but 2,000 effective soldiers (1,800 being too ill to fight) and good water to last only two or three days. If relief came quickly, he would attempt to withstand a siege, but he knew that without water, the troops could not hold out for long.[62]

Unfortunately for Doxat and his men, assistance was nowhere in sight: just a few days earlier Seckendorf, assuming that the campaigning season had ended and that Nish could endure any siege, had ordered his troops to their winter quarters on the Sava River.[63] In conjunction with this decision, Khevenhüller's corps withdrew from its observation post above Vidin, and the units in Wallachia fell back to secure positions in Transylvania, thus leaving Doxat essentially alone to face the full might of the Turks.[64] Aware of his isolation and convinced that no army would relieve him, Doxat, after discussing the situation with his officers, decided to surrender.[65] On October 16, following a Turkish promise of safe conduct to Belgrade for himself and his men, he relinquished the keys of the fortress to Ahmed Kiuprili.[66] With the surrender of Nish, the only remaining Austrian conquest of 1737 vanished and the campaign came to an unofficial close.

61 Brown, "Türkenkrieg," 1737, p. 432. By retaking Nish, Ahmed Kiuprili, the great-grandson of Mohammed Kiuprili and the tenth prominent Ottoman official of that famous name, effected the last great feat of arms of the Kiuprili family.
62 *Ibid.*, 433, Appendix SSS.
63 Angeli, "Krieg mit der Pforte," 320.
64 Brown, "Türkenkrieg," 1737, p. 419.
65 The statements of Doxat's officers can be found in *ibid.*, Appendices PPP and QQQ.
66 *Ibid.*, Appendix RRR.

Distressed by the incredibly poor showing of Austrian arms in general and the loss of Nish in particular, the Conference and the *Hofkriegsrat* began the search for those responsible for these misfortunes. Doxat, the most obvious, was selected first by the war ministry; with dispatch it accused him of cowardice, held an investigation of his conduct, sentenced him to death, and duly executed him in Belgrade in March, 1738.[67] Not satisfied with as minor a figure as Doxat, however, the Conference sought a more prominent scapegoat and marked Seckendorf the real villain. Even as the Turks invested Nish, the emperor ordered the commander in chief to relinquish his post to Field Marshal Philippi and to come to Vienna to answer accusations of incompetency.[68] Although advised by his friends to flee to Prussia, Seckendorf preferred to face the trial he knew awaited him and so returned to the capital. Upon arriving he found himself under house arrest and subjected to harassment by the populace of the city, particularly the Jesuits, who believed his disgrace an example of divine punishment for his Protestant beliefs. From the pulpit of St. Stephen's, a famous Jesuit preacher, Father Peikhart, railed, "that a heretical general at the head of a

67 Charges, testimony, and decisions by the judges concerning Doxat can be found in a lengthy collection entitled simply Appendix YYY in the campaign of 1737 in Brown's "Türkenkrieg." I used microfilm of these records rather than the book as they are listed in the *Kriegsarchiv*, where they and the evidence concerning the other officers brought to trial can be found under the title "Untersuchungsakten über General Doxat, FM Graf von Seckendorf, FM Graf Wallis, und FZM Graf Neipperg." Doxat was sentenced because the court concluded that he had plenty of artillery, ammunition, and provisions, and should have at least attempted resistance before surrendering. In addition to Doxat's conviction, each of his officers received various punishments for not having spoken in favor of making a stand against the Ottomans. For a study of Doxat's case see A., "Marginalien zu dem Aufsätze 'Nikolaus Doxat, ein Officer des Prinzen Eugenius und ein Opfer des damaligen Hofkriegsrathes' " *Mitteilungen des k.k. Kriegsarchivs* (1881), 239–46.

68 Brown, "Türkenkrieg," 1737, pp. 428–29.

Catholic army could only insult the Almighty and turn his benediction away from the arms of his Imperial and Catholic Majesty." [69]

At the hearings examining his behavior, the field marshal listened to charges not only of ineffectiveness in command but also of conspiracy to steal provisions from the commissariat to sell to the men at a personal profit. The latter indictment, eventually proven without foundation, had arisen from rumors circulating among the men encamped at Nish alleging that, because the surrounding countryside failed to yield adequate foodstuffs, Seckendorf planned to withhold bread from the soldiers in order to market it later at inflated prices. [70] In the end the investigators could pin no real guilt upon the commander in chief, except that he exercised poor judgment, and committed him to house arrest for an unspecified period of time. Seckendorf remained confined until the death of Charles VI, after which the new sovereign, Maria Theresa, granted him a full pardon and restored all his goods and titles. [71]

Even though Seckendorf committed no deliberate act of folly, there can be little doubt that he could have prevented, or at least reduced, the misfortune of the campaign of 1737. After the conquest of Nish, he could have marched all his

69 La Lande, *Histoire de l'empereur Charles VI*, IV, 577.
70 Brown, "Türkenkrieg," 1737, Appendix ZZZ. As in Doxat's case, these manuscript volumes contain the charges and testimony regarding Seckendorf's hearings. The investigation began February 21, and ended April 10, 1738, and was held before a board composed of Field Marshal Count John Harrach, two generals, and two officials from the *Hofkriegsrat*. Despite the flood of testimony, the only summary of the case was a lengthy, noncommittal memorandum written by a General Sterndahl and submitted to the *Hofkriegsrat* on May 17, 1738. For Seckendorf's case see Brown, "Türkenkrieg," 1737, Appendices ZZZ–NNNN.
71 *Ibid.*, 1737, p. 528. Seckendorf never recovered from this disgrace and, after his pardon, joined the service of Charles Albert of Bavaria, later Charles VII and a famous enemy of the House of Habsburg.

forces northward to besiege Vidin while it lay weak and improperly defended; alternatively, he could have readied his army to battle the Ottomans when they launched their offensive to retake Nish. By foregoing his expedition to Bosnia, he might have had the opportunity to force a climactic encounter as Prince Eugene had done at Zenta in 1697 and at Belgrade in 1717. In deciding to assist Hildburghausen just as the Turks began to advance, however, he found himself and his troops enmeshed in the defiles of Bosnia, too far away to pursue that decisive battle or to relieve Nish.

Seckendorf's disgrace and the dissolution of the congress of Nemirov marked the end of the Austrian military and diplomatic efforts begun in 1736. Their maneuverings had met with mixed success. On the one hand, Vienna had achieved its principal objective: the Austro-Russian alliance was still sound and appeared as though it would remain that way. In fact, despite the disappointments of 1737, as early as September both St. Petersburg and Vienna voiced the need for closer cooperation in the campaign of 1738.[72] Likewise, no longer did the councillors need worry about a Russian threat to Moldavia and Wallachia, for the extent of Münnich's losses at Ochakov precluded a major thrust into the Balkans for at least another year.

Militarily Austria seemed in relatively good condition because the army had actually suffered few casualties, experienced no substantial defeats, and given up no Austrian territory. Indeed, the chief victim was Austrian pride. As Charles wrote to his ministers abroad: "The expense, the abandonment of Nish, and the loss of more easily won advantages

72 *Referat* of the *Staatskanzlei*, September 20, 1737, in HHSA, SK, Türkei, 216; Hohenholz to Sinzendorf, September 21, 1737, in *ibid.*, Russland, II, 16. Hohenholz served as minister in Ostein's absence.

does not hurt us so much as the painful blow which the honor of our arms has endured in the eyes of the world." [73]

Vienna had, however, failed notably in one respect: it could not end the war. Aware of the pressure an extensive conflict would exert on the already heavily burdened Austrian finances and manpower, the emperor's advisers had agreed in 1736 that the struggle should last only one year; by October, however, they all realized the inevitability of at least one more year of hostilities. Fearing that another campaign would overtax Austrian resources and at the same time expose the emperor to potential threats in western Europe, the Conference knew that, even though it must prepare for a continued struggle, it also must seek to resume negotiations with the Turks by whatever means it could find.

73 *Referat* to all ministers, November 23, 1737, in *ibid.*, 134.

VI

❧ Friction Between Allies

After the conclusion of the campaign and the collapse of the congress of Nemirov, the most important task facing Vienna was to maintain contacts with the Turks in order to keep the peace talks going. Although virtually resigned to the idea of fighting at least one more year, the Conference still clung to the hope that, by convincing the Turks it wanted a settlement without territorial gain and by persuading the Russians to accept minimal border revisions, it might effect an armistice without expending much more blood and treasure.[1]

Shortly following the fall of Nish, the desired channel of communication opened when a messenger from the pasha of Bosnia asked Field Marshal Philippi to send someone to the frontier to discuss an agreement based on the Treaty of Passarowitz.[2] Seizing this opportunity to reopen the dialogue, Vienna chose Nicholas Theil, a military officer and official translator, to meet with the pasha. His instructions were to

1 Bartenstein to emperor, November 24, 1737, in HHSA, SK, Vorträge, 47.
2 Bartenstein to emperor, October 25, 1737, *ibid.*

118

express the emperor's willingness to use Passarowitz as a foundation for peace, but to emphasize that all discussions must include representatives from Russia. When Theil delivered this message, the pasha insisted that only a bilateral exchange of views without Russian participation would bring peace.[3]

The pasha's reply greatly disturbed the councillors because it forced them to consider a question they had hoped to avoid. Should the emperor grant priority to the securing of peace or to the maintenance of the Russian alliance? Fortunately, the Habsburg advisers did not have to answer this question, at least for the time being, for in mid-November they learned that the king of France had offered to mediate. Greatly relieved by this development, the Conference knew that if all parties accepted the king's services, in any future negotiations diplomatic protocol would demand that the French treat Russia and Austria as indivisible allies. Thus convinced that French arbitration would keep the Austro-Russian union intact and hopeful that the recent signs of French friendship would make Paris sympathetic to Vienna's wishes, the Conference embraced the king's offer and set out to encourage St. Petersburg and Constantinople to do the same.[4]

Although the Austrians did not realize it, more stood behind this French strategem than merely the wish to end the discord in southeastern Europe. Despite his refusal to become militarily involved, Cardinal Fleury had retained an intense interest in this war, especially its impact on the Austro-Russian accord. Ever since the appearance of the empress' troops in Germany during the War of the Polish Succession, this alliance had disturbed him deeply; and he worried that in the

3 Report of the conversation between Nicholas Theil and the Pasha of Bosnia in Theil to Philippi, November 30, 1737, in *ibid.*, Russland, II, 134.
4 Bartenstein to emperor, November 4, 1737, in *ibid.*, Vorträge, 47.

future Vienna might use its associate's forces again and again to exert its power in western Europe. In 1739 he best expressed his concern by writing that the concert between Russia and Austria was "a very dangerous thing. One has seen in the affairs of Poland what abuse the court of Vienna can make of this alliance, and if it can bring 10,000 Muscovites to the Rhine, in other circumstances it would be able to inundate Germany with barbarian troops, when it deems it necessary to force the Empire to its will." [5]

Furthermore, the cardinal feared that this coalition might eclipse for some time French influence in eastern Europe. Having already subjected Poland to their will, in the summer of 1737 Austria and Russia seemed on the brink of inflicting a defeat on the Ottoman Empire that would virtually eliminate it as a great power. In early autumn, before news had reached Paris of the Ottoman reconquest of Nish and the withdrawal of the Austro-Russian armies from the field, Fleury's foreign minister wrote: "Today . . . Ochakov is in the hands of the Muscovites, the entrance to the Crimea is open to them; the Emperor . . . is engaged in the war and almost all of Wallachia and Moldavia have submitted to him. By taking Nish, he has become the master of all of Serbia. A second campaign will yield to his arms and to those of the Empress all that the Ottoman Empire possesses in Europe." [6] Contemplating the distasteful possibility that additional Turkish defeats would prostrate all of eastern Europe before Vienna and St. Petersburg, Fleury decided that he must either break up the Austro-Russian alliance or at least render it ineffective.

Before he had turned to the idea of mediation, the cardinal

[5] Instructions to Marquis de la Chetardie, July 1, 1739, *Recueil des instructions*, I, 344.
[6] Amelot to Villeneuve, October 18, 1737, in HHSA, SK, Russland, II, 134.

had at first sought to use his newly established amity with the Habsburg court to foment suspicion of Russia. In a personal letter to Charles VI (which the Austrians passed to Ostermann), he warned the emperor to beware of Russian aggrandizement because it could lead to the Muscovite conquest of the Crimea, domination of the Black Sea, and the blockade of Constantinople itself. The end result would be the disruption of European commerce in the Levant and the collapse of the balance of power in eastern Europe. To avoid these unwanted results, Charles should content himself with minor annexations in Bosnia, abandon his formidable associate, and conclude peace, "without thinking of destroying entirely the Turkish Empire in Europe." [7]

Although voicing thanks for this message, the emperor had appeared singularly unimpressed with its dire forecast, so Fleury turned to mediation as his tactic for applying pressure to the alliance. By controlling the peace negotiations and using his influence to bring all the belligerents to a settlement, he believed that he could preserve Turkey's integrity, retain Austria's friendship, and blunt Russia's penetration into southeastern Europe. To perform this task would require great diplomatic skill, but the cardinal had complete confidence that he and the man he selected as official mediator, Ambassador Villeneuve, had an excellent chance of succeeding.

Winning the belligerents' approval of French arbitration seemed an easy matter to Fleury, for, as early as July, 1737, he had received a formal solicitation for French intervention from the grand vizier, who apparently already believed that the congress of Nemirov would end in failure. Convinced by this bid that the sultan would pose no obstacle and certain that the emperor would do virtually anything to end the war

7 Cardinal Fleury to Charles VI, August 19, 1737, in *ibid.*, Türkei, 216.

quickly, Fleury saw only the Russians as possible opponents to his mediation.[8] Instead of approaching the empress himself, however, he simply turned the task of wooing her over to the Austrians.[9] After all, the Russians would more likely listen to their allies than to an uncertain neutral.

The emperor willingly accepted the task of persuading his friends largely because Bartenstein felt that he would have little difficulty convincing them of the efficacy of French mediation. Sobered by the events of 1737, they should, he believed, have abandoned their grandiose designs and be more interested in working out a reasonable and prompt settlement. To induce them to approve of Fleury's initiative, however, Bartenstein avoided mentioning their recent military reversals. He preferred instead to argue that French mediation would be best for all because France alone possessed sufficient influence to compel the Turks to accept a settlement, prevent western pressure on Austria, and especially discourage the Swedes from attacking Russia. Drawing particular attention to this last argument, the secretary told of persistent rumors in European court circles that a war party hoped to convince the next Swedish Diet to capitalize upon Russia's involvement in the south and regain some of the Baltic provinces lost to St. Petersburg in the Great Northern War. The empress could avoid a two-front war with Turkey and Sweden, Bartenstein advised, if, before the Diet met in 1738, she would only adopt French mediation and moderate her demands for territorial compensation.[10]

To Bartenstein's surprise the Russians did not receive his

8 Cardinal Fleury to grand vizier, October 17, 1737, in *ibid.*, Russland, II, 134.

9 Vandal, *Une ambassade française*, 291; Laugier, *Histoire des négociations*, I, 73.

10 Emperor to Hohenholz, November 8, 1737, and emperor to Ostein and Talman, November 8, 1737, in HHSA, SK, Russland, II, 134.

proposal with the equanimity he expected. Ostein reported that, upon seeing Fleury's August letter to the emperor, Ostermann had felt so outraged by its bias that he had persuaded the empress to issue a manifesto repudiating its insinuations.[11] Furthermore, the foreign minister implied that Vienna's planned acceptance of this obviously anti-Russian cardinal's mediation, coming concurrently with rumors that the Austrians had already met clandestinely with the pasha of Bosnia, seemed to mean that the emperor planned to desert his ally for a separate settlement with the Turks.[12]

At this time Ostermann had good reason to fear Austrian intentions because, not only did the diplomatic situation appear to be swaying against Russia's interests, but the military scene as well. Just as Ostein presented his master's suggestions for French mediation, news came that the Turks were besieging the dearly won fortress of Ochakov. Instead of following the unwritten eighteenth-century rule of retiring to winter quarters at the beginning of autumn, Ottoman forces numbering 20,000 regulars and 20,000 Tartars had launched a general assault on the fortress in early November in order to win it back for the sultan. Their chances appeared good, for Münnich had warned from the Ukraine that a relief force could not reach the beleaguered garrison for several weeks and in the meantime the fortress might fall.[13] Coming at the

11 Manifesto of the empress in Ostein to emperor, November 26, 1737, in *ibid.*, 16.

12 *Anweisung* to Ostein and Talman, October 26, 1737, in *ibid.*, Türkei, 217. This instruction ordered the two envoys to inform the Russians of the border talks and to assure them that nothing would be done contrary to the Austro-Russian convention. In fact the Russians themselves were not entirely innocent of seeking a separate settlement. In August, Ostermann had authorized Nepluyev to suggest private talks with the Turks at Nemirov, but the envoy received no encouraging response. Uebersberger, *Russlands Orientpolitik*, 205–207.

13 Hohenholz to Sinzendorf, November 26, 1737, in HHSA, SK, Russland, II, 16.

same time, the Austrian note and the reports from the field upset Ostermann noticeably; all his dreams of conquest seemed about to shatter. Expressing his rage to Ostein's assistant, Count Hohenholz, he heatedly ridiculed the emperor's "one-sided acceptance" of Fleury's mediation and complained that Vienna wished only to sacrifice Russia's bravely won victories for its own advantage.[14]

This mood of depression on Ostermann's part lasted only briefly, for in early December reports arrived in the Russian capital that the Ochakov garrison had successfully withstood the Turkish onslaught and had forced the enemy to retire.[15] Although congratulating St. Petersburg on its success, the Conference actually registered some disappointment over the Ottoman withdrawal because it had hoped that Turkish pressure on Ochakov would compel Ostermann to fall into step with Vienna's search for a settlement.[16]

The councillors had little time to reflect on this disappointment, for soon Vienna found itself on the receiving end of a vigorous Russian diplomatic offensive that seemed designed not only to undermine the emperor's peace efforts but also to place Austria in some danger. His confidence apparently restored by the successful defense of Ochakov, Ostermann set out to impress upon the emperor that St. Petersburg would retain its freedom of action and would not have to submit to any deals Austria made on its own. As his first step, he announced the empress' acceptance of French mediation, but only on the condition that Britain and Holland be recruited as co-arbi-

14 Hohenholz to Sinzendorf, November 30, 1737, *ibid.*

15 Hohenholz to emperor, December 2, 1737, *ibid.* After a series of unsuccessful attempts to storm the fortress, the Turks, suffering from a constant downpour of rain and enormous casualties, abandoned the siege on November 10, 1737. Hohenholz reported that, upon hearing of the successful defense of Ochakov, the Russians rejoiced more than they had upon hearing of its capture.

16 Bartenstein to emperor, December 17, 1737, in *ibid.* Vorträge, 47.

trators. Undoubtedly aware of the unfriendly relations between Paris and the seapowers, he knew that this proviso would either reduce Fleury's influence on the negotiations or force him to withdraw from them altogether.[17]

This act disturbed the Habsburg policy makers considerably, but, before they could recover, they learned that Ostermann had also opened semisecret negotiations with the Turks through the pasha of Ochakov, whom the Russians had captured when they stormed the fortress in mid-July. Actually the Ottomans themselves had suggested the talks, for in mid-October the pasha had received a note from the grand vizier authorizing him to begin discussions with his captors concerning a separate peace.[18] Nonetheless Ostermann's willingness to engage in such discussions so soon after his hearing of Austria's contacts with the pasha of Bosnia indicated that the Russian foreign minister wanted to show Vienna that he could play the same clandestine game of hidden diplomacy that the Austrians had inaugurated.

While the Conference still reeled from these two Russian ploys, it learned of a third, which instantly became far more serious than the previous two: Russia appeared willing to open negotiations with Prussia concerning the problem of suc-

17 Ostermann might have believed that he could keep Ochakov if the seapowers mediated the dispute. In mid-October the Russian minister at the Hague suggested to Horatio Walpole that, if Britain arbitrated, it would perhaps allow St. Petersburg to retain both Azov and Ochakov. Although Walpole replied that Britain would insist upon the return of Ochakov to the Turks, speculation persisted that the seapowers would allow the Russians to preserve all their conquests. Ulfeld to emperor, November 16, 1737, in HHSA, SK, Russland, II, 134.

18 Rondeau to Harrington, November 19, 1737, *Sbornik*, LXXX, 227–28; Hohenholz to Sinzendorf, December 24, 1737, in HHSA, SK, Russland, II, 16. Some time later, Ostermann informed Fleury that he had presented the pasha with "neither a project for peace nor preliminary articles, but only certain propositions related to a particular settlement." Ostermann to Fleury, April 22, 1738, *Sbornik*, LXXXVI, 10.

cession in the west German provinces of Jülich and Berg. Situated along the lower Rhine River and possessing immense strategic and economic value, these two provinces had been the focus of controversy since the middle of the seventeenth century, when they were awarded to the Palatine-Neuberg family over the claims of the Prussian House of Hohenzollern. Although the Hohenzollerns had received the neighboring lands of Cleves and Mark at the same time, they did not abandon their desire to secure Jülich-Berg as well. In 1736 the ruler of Jülich-Berg, Charles Philip, was old, infirm, and without male issue. Frederick William I revived his family's pretentions in hopes of winning the provinces over the claims of Charles Philip's closest relatives, the Palatine-Sulzbachs. In an effort to avoid a confrontation between the two competing houses, Austria, Britain, France, and the Netherlands opened collective discussions to determine who should succeed the aged prince when he died.[19]

Even though it agreed to submit the succession problem to the arbitration of the four powers, Berlin feared that they would award the two provinces to the rival Palatine-Sulzbachs out of a sense of distrust of Prussia's growing power. To guard against such an eventuality, in the autumn of 1737 the king of Prussia offered St. Petersburg a military alliance, by which the Prussians promised to assist Russia in its struggle with the Turks in exchange for Russian recognition of Hohenzollern claims to Jülich-Berg and a pledge to help the king secure the provinces.[20] While Ostermann agreed to examine this proposal, Biron reported it to Ostein and requested the emperor's comments.[21]

19 Johann Gustav Droysen, *Geschichte der preussischen Politik* (Leipzig, 1870), IV, 288–89.
20 For the Jülich-Berg question from the Prussian point-of-view, see *ibid.*, 271–364.
21 Hohenholz to emperor, November 16, 1737, in HHSA, SK, Russland, II, 16.

As the Russian foreign minister undoubtedly surmised, nothing disturbed the Habsburg court more than the prospect of a Russo-Prussian rapprochement. Vienna had harbored strong suspicions of Prussia since the War of the Polish Succession, when Berlin, although promising to assist the emperor with 50,000 men, sent only 10,000 to the imperial camp and left the rest poised on the borders of Jülich-Berg, ready to pounce should the ruler die. Believing that at any moment Berlin might take advantage of Austria's involvement in the Turkish war to annex the two provinces, the Conference felt that Prussia constituted a serious threat to Habsburg interests in northern Germany. In early 1738 Bartenstein revealed the general distrust of Prussia with a comment of great portent for his and Austria's future. To the emperor he wrote: "There is no lack of people who advise the King of Prussia to turn his military might away from Jülich-Berg and direct it against Silesia and Bohemia." [22] Shortly before, he had advised Hohenholz to stress to the Russian court that, "the Emperor has no greater enemy than the King of Prussia." [23]

All of these diplomatic maneuvers on Ostermann's part— his balking at French mediation, his exchanges with the pasha of Ochakov, and his flirtation with Prussia's overtures

22 Bartenstein to emperor, April 5, 1738, in *ibid.*, Vorträge, 47. As a result of the negotiations at the Hague, on February 10, 1738, the four powers presented to the king of Prussia identical notes suggesting that, if the ruler of Jülich-Berg should die, the prince of Sulzbach would occupy the two duchies pending a final decision of the four powers. Frederick William rejected this plan and marched 40,000 men into the Hohenzollern province of Cleves, which bordered both disputed lands. In reply Fleury ordered the French minister of war to reinforce the units along the Rhine in order to repulse a Prussian invasion should Berlin choose to settle the issue by force. The crisis subsided without incident, however, when Frederick William agreed that, when the sovereign of the two duchies died, neutral troops, half-Catholic and half-Protestant, should occupy both duchies.

23 Emperor to Hohenholz, February 20, 1738, in *ibid.*, Russland, II, 135.

—frightened the Conference into breaking off its own independent discussions with the Turks and begging the Russian foreign minister to reject all thoughts of a Russo-Prussian accord. The abandonment of the separate talks and the pleading tone the Austrians adopted concerning Russia's attitudes toward Prussia obviously pleased Ostermann, for he soon terminated his associations with Berlin and Constantinople and even accepted French arbitration without insisting upon British and Dutch participation.[24] Apparently not really serious about pursuing any of these diplomatic thrusts, Ostermann seemed to have used them only to express his displeasure at Vienna's private contacts with Fleury and the pasha of Bosnia and to emphasize that he did not have to consent to any arrangements Vienna might make without first consulting him.

Despite the Russian minister's compliance with Austrian wishes once he had impressed his freedom of action upon Vienna, his diplomatic fencing had irritated Bartenstein immeasurably. Convinced that Ostermann had engaged in all these maneuvers merely to sabotage Vienna's efforts to restore peace, the secretary believed that, if he could only undermine Ostermann's influence at the Russian court, St. Petersburg would follow the emperor's lead in dealing with the Turks and the French.[25] To achieve this goal, Bartenstein restored to the time-honored practice of court intrigue. He instructed Hohenholz to inform Biron and the empress fre-

24 In May, 1738, Biron told the Prussian minister in St. Petersburg that Berlin should abide by the decision of the great powers regarding Jülich-Berg and that the empress saw no reason to involve Russia. Ostein to emperor, May 16, 1738, in *ibid.*, 12.

25 Bartenstein believed Ostermann personally responsible for undermining hopes for peace, because in December Hohenholz reported that both Biron and the empress were willing to abandon Ochakov; but Ostermann insisted upon retaining it. Hohenholz to emperor, December 11, 1737 and Hohenholz to Sinzendorf, December 21, 1737, in *ibid.*, 16.

quently in private that Ostermann, by displaying Austro-Russian differences for all of Europe to see, had crippled efforts to reach a settlement. Hohenholz was to suggest that the only way to end this skullduggery would be to appoint another person to countersign the foreign minister's dispatches and fill the advisory councils with men independent of his influence.[26] Such controls alone would restore harmony to allied relations.[27]

Bartenstein's long-distance conspiracy continued without notable success or failure until mid-May, 1738, when it suffered a harsh blow. In a personal letter to Charles, Anne emphasized that Ostermann did not work behind her back but followed her orders in all that he did and insisted that Austrian machinations against him stop at once. Professing puzzlement at Vienna's attacks on her foreign minister, she protested both Ostermann's and her loyalty to the Austrian alliance.[28] Faced with this message and accompanying reports that Russia had broken off negotiations with the pasha of Ochakov and the Prussians, Bartenstein had no choice but to ease his attacks, at least for the time being.[29]

By May, 1738, the Austrians and Russians had patched up their quarrels and appeared ready to cooperate with the French in finding an end to the war. Even Ostermann voiced his willingness to reach a settlement, having already in February sent Villeneuve his terms, which surprisingly included the return of Ochakov to the Turks.[30] One might imagine

26 Emperor to Hohenholz, January 20, 1738, in *ibid.*, 135. To draw Biron into the anti-Ostermann camp, the emperor conferred upon him the title of "durchleuchtig," an honor immensely attractive to Biron because only the Holy Roman Emperor could present it. Emperor to Ostein, April 17, 1738, *ibid.*
27 Emperor to Hohenholz, February 26, 1738, HHSA, SK, Russland, II, 135.
28 Empress Anne to emperor, May 13, 1738, *ibid.*
29 Ostein to emperor, May 16, 1738, in *ibid.*, 17.
30 Emperor to Hohenholz, March 2, 1738, in *ibid.*, 135.

that the Russian minister, who had expressed such determination to retain this fortress in December, would have sought all possible ways to protect it; but by February his officers had informed him of its certain fall if besieged in the spring, therefore Ostermann decided to sacrifice it in order to secure the more vital bastion of Azov.[31]

The Russian willingness to concede Ochakov, coupled with Vienna's offer to reestablish the terms of the Peace of Passarowitz, should have ended the war, because these provisions corresponded exactly to the "reasonable and just" articles composed by Bartenstein on the basis of soundings taken in the other European courts. Even the mediators found them acceptable, for in December Fleury had written: "If his Imperial Majesty consents to make peace on the basis of Passarowitz and the Tsarina agrees to return Ochakov and Kinburn [Kinburn being a small bastion to the south of Ochakov], the Porte has no choice but to sign a treaty."[32] By virtue of this consensus between the allies and the arbitrator, a settlement appeared close at hand.

This time, however, the Turks repudiated the allies' offers and scorned the thought of peace altogether. Throughout the winter, while the Austrians and Russians had wasted their time in diplomatic banter, the Turks had been zealously preparing for—and at times indulging in—the continuation of hostilities. In late autumn, inspired by the reconquest of Nish and Münnich's retreat to the Ukraine, the Ottoman soldiery had dedicated itself to inflicting crushing defeats upon the infidel enemy. According to the Dutch minister, writing from the war camp of the grand vizier: "The Turks have solemnly pledged to persist in this double war with all possible vigor; everyone here favors extraordinary efforts in order to keep the Ottoman armies in action everywhere into the winter. They

31 Hohenholz to emperor, March 21, 1738, in *ibid.*, 17.
32 Schmerling to emperor, December 2, 1737, in *ibid.*, 134.

all sing only of victory." [33] True to their word, as late as November the sultan's forces struck at Habsburg units near the fortresses of Mehadia and Orsova in southern Hungary, and not until the end of the month, when the assault began on Ochakov, did these raids cease. [34]

In December, 1737, Turkish enthusiasm rose even higher because, on the advice of the Kizlar Aga, the influential black eunuch and doorkeeper of the harem, the sultan appointed Jegen (Devil) Mohammed as grand vizier. "Rough, overbearing, a fanatical Moslem, and far more inclined to war than peace," he possessed an inordinate love of combat and desire for victories, which he transmitted to the government and to the ranks of the fighting men. [35] Believing the emperor's forces weaker and more accessible than those of the empress, the new grand vizier at once determined to concentrate his efforts primarily against Austria.

As his first step in his offensive, Jegen invited Joseph Rákóczi, the symbol of anti-Habsburg feeling in Hungary, to come to Constantinople for an audience with the sultan. After the defeat of his father Francis Rákóczi, the leader of a Magyar revolt in the first decade of the eighteenth century, Joseph had been taken to Vienna and subjected to Habsburg tutors who hoped to teach him loyalty to the emperor. Their teachings failed, however, and in 1736 he fled the Austrian capital, assumed the role of Hungarian revolutionary, and traveled to the Ottoman Empire to seek aid. [36] When he first set foot on Turkish land, the Porte refused to receive him because it still desired to maintain good relations with Austria. When such hopes had evaporated by 1737, it brought him to

33 Calkoën to Bruyninx, October 7, 1737, *ibid.*
34 Angeli, "Der Krieg mit der Pforte," 331.
35 Cassels, *The Struggle for the Ottoman Empire*, 139; Joseph von Hammer-Purgstall, *Geschichte des osmanischen Reiches* (Pest, 1831), VII, 503.
36 F. Krones, "Zur Geschichte Ungarns," 78.

Constantinople, where the sultan greeted him with all the pomp and circumstance accorded heads of state.[37] One month later, Rákóczi announced a formal alliance between himself and the sultan, in which the Ottoman chief promised to help him establish an independent state of Hungary and Transylvania to act as a buffer between the Ottoman and Habsburg empires. Emphasizing that he wished not to join this new creation to the Turkish state but only "to give back to both lands their freedom and venerable constitutions," he appealed to all Magyar patriots to join his standard and promised eighty *gulden* to any brave warrior who came.[38]

When he secured the recognition of Rákóczi as head of state and signed the treaty with him, Jegen obviously had far more in mind than rebellion in Hungary or irritation to the Habsburgs; the main purpose of this fanfare was to pave the way for a military alliance with France. The Porte had desired such a pact for some time but had failed to secure one because Fleury, an upright Roman Catholic cardinal, refused to desecrate the name of the Most Christian King of France by concluding a formal agreement with the infidel. Jegen hoped that Fleury would view the Rákóczi-Ottoman arrangement as a precedent for further Moslem-Christian accords and would be far more sympathetic to the sultan's requests in the future. Thus, shortly after the announcement of the union with Rákóczi, the grand vizier requested an alliance with France.[39]

Upon receiving the Turk's appeal, Fleury still rejected the idea of a Franco-Turkish pact, but he did pledge his master's

37 For a description of his arrival, see Vandal, *Une ambassade française*, 318ff.
38 Manifesto of Joseph Rákóczi, January 28, 1738; and Proclamation of Joseph Rákóczi, January 30, 1739, in HHSA, SK, Türkei, 218.
39 Heinrich Benedikt, "Die europäische Politik der Pforte vor Beginn und während des österreichischen Erbfolgekrieges," *Mitteilungen des österreichischen Staatsarchivs*, I (1948), 149.

guarantee for any formal treaty concluded between Turkey and its opponents.[40] This meant that France would apply pressure to any party that violated the final settlement and compel it to abide by the conditions of the agreement. Although by no means a military accord, this guarantee must have pleased Jegen considerably, for it marked the first time that a Christian power vowed to safeguard the integrity of the Ottoman Empire.[41]

When hearing of Rákóczi's accommodation with the sultan, Vienna naturally disregarded its implications for Turkish-French relations and sought to minimize the impact it might have among the dissident elements in Hungary. The emperor immediately branded the Magyar leader a *Hauptrebel*, proclaimed all who joined him traitors, and offered a reward of 10,000 *gulden* to anyone who captured him alive and 6,000 to anyone who brought him in dead. Men who had followed him but assisted in his arrest would receive a full pardon.[42] Superficially these Habsburg manifestos appeared to have served their purpose because almost no Magyars enlisted in Rákóczi's cause. Actually, however, not the Austrian threats, of which the Hungarian noblemen had seen and ignored many, but Joseph's own unfamiliarity with his countrymen defeated his purpose. Although they loved his father, few Magyars felt any affinity for the son, whom they had never seen as an adult but who they believed, "had not the genius, insight, or virtue of his father for undertaking and sustaining a campaign of such importance and delicacy." [43]

40 Fleury to grand vizier, April 10, 1738, in HHSA, SK, Türkei, 218.

41 Vandal, *Une ambassade française*, 327. The first formal treaty between Turkey and a Christian power was the Turko-Swedish alliance of July 19, 1740. Benedikt, "Die europäische Politik," 158.

42 Manifesto of the emperor, April 28, 1738, in HHSA, SK, Russland, II, 136.

43 César de Saussure, *Lettres de Turquie, 1730–1739 et notices, 1740* (Budapest, 1909), 181.

Consequently, ignored by his countrymen and fearful of assassination by a Habsburg agent, Rákóczi lived in terror until November, 1738, when he died "some said of the plague, others of a malignant fever, and still others of poison." [44] With the Turks so obviously intent upon continuing the war, by mid-spring the Austrians and Russians abandoned their halting search for a settlement and focused their attention fully on preparations for the upcoming campaign. As early as October, 1737, the allies had begun to debate operations plans, but unfortunately these talks simply followed the established pattern. As in the year before, the Russians, to avoid any Austrian restrictions on their designs, announced a non-negotiable strategy; their armies would besiege the fortress of Bendery on the lower Dniester and invade the Crimea.[45] The Habsburg officers could respond to this declaration only by uttering a few insults about Russian military prowess, dispatching another officer to St. Petersburg to try to talk Russian headquarters into investing Khotin, and, finally, reluctantly accepting their ally's proposal.[46]

Feeling abandoned for the second consecutive year, Vienna turned to the task of readying its own forces for the Turkish onslaught it feared would certainly come. To refit the army appeared a much more difficult operation than it had been in 1737, for illness had taken a severe toll of the men during

44 *Ibid.*
45 Hohenholz to emperor, February 6, 1738, in HHSA, SK, Russland, II, 17.
46 The officer assigned to this task was Marquis Botha d'Adorno, who arrived in the Russian capital on February 21, 1738. Although he soon discovered that his mission was futile, he remained in Russia and persevered in the hopeless job of trying to convince Münnich to march on Khotin. Botha to Emperor, March 1, 1738, *ibid.* Botha's instructions can be found in *ibid.*, 206. The Austrian officers accused the Russians of indulging in only a "four-day" campaign (the siege of Ochakov) in 1737 and agreed that Münnich was an incompetent commander in chief. Emperor to Hohenholz, November 8, 1737, in *ibid.*, 134.

the winter. Rather than the normal 600 to 800 men, most of the battalions numbered between 300 and 400 and a few contained only 200; all of the fortresses, including the two strongpoints of Belgrade and Petrovaradin, had garrisons far below their usual strength.[47] To make good these deficiencies, the *Hofkriegsrat* had to scour the land for recruits while the *Hofkammer* introduced a special poll tax to equip and remunerate them.[48] Notwithstanding these efforts, by June the army consisted of only 22,840 foot and 11,654 horse, a total apparently inadequate to repulse the rumored 60,000 regulars the Turks were collecting to send against them.[49]

As the *Hofkriegsrat* and the *Hofkammer* tried to gather the necessary men and money, Charles tackled the problem of choosing a new commander in chief. Wishing this time to avoid the factionalism that followed the appointment of Seckendorf, the emperor selected an essentially noncontroversial figure, his son-in-law, Francis Stephen of Lorraine. Although Francis Stephen had no military experience aside from his junket as a "volunteer" in 1737, by naming him, Charles hoped to minimize intrigue among the general officers and, at the same time, give his son-in-law the opportunity to "win the people" by defeating the Turks.[50]

47 Brown, "Türkenkrieg," 1738, Appendix X. In addition to malaria, the plague infected the army in 1738 and 1739. According to Brown, in May, 1738, two cavalry battalions were withdrawn from Transylvania to reinforce units in the Banat; one of these supposedly carried the disease, which it had contracted from some Rumanian noblemen fleeing the Turks in Moldavia. Brown, "Türkenkrieg," 1738, p. 39. Plague, not the Turks, became the scourge of the Austrian army in its final two campaigns of this war.
48 La Lande, *Histoire de l'empereur Charles VI*, V, 21.
49 Brown, "Türkenkrieg," 1738, pp. 73–79, 110–11.
50 The campaign of 1738 scarcely enhanced Lorraine's prestige among the people. After it ended, he and his wife moved to Florence to assume the duties of rulers of Tuscany and to avoid any outbursts against him in Vienna. Fred Hennings, *Und sitzet zur linken Hand: Franz Stephan von Lothringen* (Vienna, 1961), 192.

Despite his desire to embellish his son-in-law's reputation, Charles naturally had no intention of trusting his fortunes to such an untried young man; thus, while leaving Francis in nominal command, he gave the real authority to the president of the *Hofkriegsrat*, Count Königsegg. Handsome, tactful, and a lover of the good life, the count's contributions to the House of Habsburg before 1738 had resulted largely from his diplomatic, not his military, prowess. His great moment had come in 1725, when, as minister to Spain, he played a major role in engineering the downfall of the Spanish favorite, Ripperda, and thus easing Vienna's later withdrawal from the Austro-Spanish alliance.[51] His capacity as a general, however, fell short of his ambassadorial talent, and, as commander in chief of the Austrian forces in Italy in 1734–1735, he had earned a reputation for failing to pursue his advantages and for exaggerating the difficulty of strategic problems facing him.[52] Of him one eighteenth-century historian wrote:

> Certainly knowledgable of details, he understood very well the parts of the whole; he knew perfectly the use of garrison troops; he was quite capable of commanding in one place. But the order of march of armies, choice of positions, the grand maneuvers of attack and retreat were foreign to him. His orders, always replete with minutiae, were obscure. The principal precautions escaped him, and preparations for conducting grand strategy meant nothing to him.[53]

Despite his thus-far unimpressive performances in the field, Königsegg was, after all, president of the war ministry, and Charles had little doubt his new commander in chief would

51 Arneth, *Prinz Eugen*, III, 217–18; Muret, *Prépondérance anglaise*, 172.
52 Arneth, *Prinz Eugen*, III, 445–46.
53 [?] de Keralio, *Histoire de la guerre des Russes et des Impériaux contre les Turcs* (Paris, 1780), II, 45–46.

achieve for himself, his emperor, and Francis Stephen a certain measure of success.

When in June the Austrian army under its new chiefs began operations, it found itself already on the defensive. In their enthusiasm to destroy the Christian forces, the Turks had initiated their offensive in January. By February they had ravaged much of Habsburg Wallachia and Serbia, by May had taken the two minor fortifications of Uzice and Mehadia, and by June had invested the important island-fortress of New Orsova in the Danube.[54] To relieve this fortress rather than to besiege Vidin became the immediate objective of the Habsburg troops, because its fall would render operations down the Danube impossible.[55]

While marching to this beleaguered bastion, on July 4 the Austrians encountered a major Turkish force at the village of Cornea, about 30 miles north of New Orsova. In the ensuing struggle, the imperial troops inflicted such a resounding defeat upon their enemy that the Turks, leaving their stores and artillery behind, not only fled the field of combat, but abandoned Mehadia, lifted the siege of New Orsova, and hastily retreated southward into Serbia.[56] When the news of the victory reached Vienna, the city and court celebrated joyously; they praised the feats of the officers and men and, upon learning that Francis Stephen had issued orders calmly under fire, hailed him as a second Prince Eugene.[57]

54 Brown, "Türkenkrieg," 1738, pp. 26–66.
55 Angeli, "Der Krieg mit der Pforte," 420. This fortress withstood the siege well, partly because the Turkish commander chose to break it down with artillery rather than by storm and partly because the commander of the fortress, Colonel Correnberg, planned to fight to the last man. Recalling the fate of Doxat, Correnberg explained that he "would rather be buried in the ruins of the place than surrender it."
56 Brown, "Türkenkrieg," 1738, pp. 116–23.
57 Arneth, *Geschichte Maria Theresia's*, I, 43. Part of this enthusiasm was directed against Seckendorf, living in Vienna under house arrest since October, 1737, when a mob assaulted his house,

Vienna's euphoria, however, was short lived. No sooner
had Königsegg routed the Turks at Cornea, than he learned
of the approach of another Ottoman army under the personal
command of the grand vizier and, in order to avoid contact,
ordered a general retreat. His subordinates openly protested
the decision, arguing that the commander in chief should seek
a climactic battle as Prince Eugene had done, but Königsegg's
mind could not be changed.[58] Not even a second major success
over the Turks near Mehadia could alter his resolution; he
retired his men farther up the Danube and abandoned both
Mehadia and New Orsova to the enemy.[59]

After reports of nothing but victories, the news of Königsegg's retreat completely bewildered the court of Vienna.
With such a glorious record and such bright prospects for
continuing progress, how could the army withdraw? Unable
to answer this question except by blaming the commander in
chief's incompetence, Charles decided to remove Königsegg
and invest his son-in-law with effective, as well as titular,
authority to command.[60] Shortly after the appropriate orders
were composed, however, a seriously ill Francis Stephen
suddenly arrived in the capital, therefore the emperor allowed Königsegg to remain in command until the troops
entered winter quarters.[61]

---

broke windows, and shouted abusive names. Not until a detachment of
cavalry arrived and spirited him and his family away did the violence
cease. Sinzendorf to Ostein, July 23, 1738, in HHSA, SK, Russland,
II, 136.

58 In a military conference held on July 11, four of the officers,
Neipperg, Hildburghausen, Wallis, and Seher, counseled some form of
pursuit of the enemy; two—Philippi, who felt cavalry fodder too
scarce for an offensive, and Königsegg—favored retreat. Brown
"Türkenkrieg," 1738, pp. 128–31.

59 In this encounter the Austrians captured 33 enemy flags, 2
kettledrums, and a large drum belonging to the Janissary corps. *Ibid.*,
137–39.

60 Emperor to Francis Stephan, July 23, 1738, *ibid.*, 145–46.

61 *Ibid.*, 159.

The midsummer battles of Cornea and Mehadia marked the only action of 1738, for well into the autumn the commander in chief avoided conflict at all possible cost. Although enduring slight battle casualties, the Habsburg forces sustained withering losses in health and morale. By marching and bivouacking in the marshes of the Danubian valley, the soldiers grew more and more tired and increasing numbers became ill. Within a short time, sickness had struck so many men that, to prevent its spread, headquarters ordered the building of special camps for the infected 1,000 paces from the healthy troops and the burning of all clothing, tents, and personal possessions of the dead.[62] Soon disease affected operations to the point of rendering reconaissance patrols impossible and forcing Vienna to dispatch 400 officers of all grades from other parts of the empire to make up losses in leadership.[63]

By October the campaign had ended, like the one of the year before, in great disappointment. This time the Austrians had achieved some victories but had seen them frittered away by the timidity of their commander in chief. Not only had this officer failed to pursue his advantages, but his religious avoidance of all action after the two battles had resulted only in a disheartened, distraught, and diseased body of men.

After such a dismal showing on its part, Vienna could only hope that its ally had in some way compensated for its deficiencies, but indeed the Russians had fared no better. Starting out for the Turkish fortress of Bendery, Münnich's forces, in order to cross the forbidding steppe, had loaded themselves down with such an enormous supply of food and fodder that the march slowed to a crawl. Consequently, not until mid-

62 Keralio, *Histoire de la guerre*, II, 93–94. In September, 1738, an officer reported that an estimated 30 to 40 men in the field army alone were dying daily from disease. Brown, "Türkenkrieg," 1738, pp. 287–88.
63 Angeli, "Der Krieg mit der Pforte," 435.

August did they reach the Dniester, where they discovered an army of some 60,000 Turks and Tartars waiting for them on the opposite bank. Fearing that his exhausted men could not achieve a victory against a well-entrenched enemy and believing a defeat would end in a wild and disastrous flight across the hostile steppe, Münnich decided to forego an encounter and ordered his men to withdraw. Having consumed most of its provisions, the army could not retrace the way it had come and had to return to Russia via neutral Poland. The other portion of the campaign, Lacy's invasion of the Crimea, followed the familiar pattern of 1736 and 1737; after destroying a few villages and running out of supplies, Lacy turned back without achieving notable success.[64] The one significant event of the Russian operations was the evacuation and razing of the dearly won fortresses of Ochakov and Kinburn, both garrisons having suffered severely from the plague. Ochakov alone cost Russia 20,000 lives.[65]

64 Manstein, *Contemporary Memoirs*, 199–212.
65 *Ibid.*, 217.

VII

❦ The Urge
for Peace

By late September, 1738, Austrian fortunes appeared to have reached their nadir; New Orsova had fallen, mighty Timişoara was threatened, illness raged through the army, and an advantageous peace seemed impossible to achieve. With these conditions worsening, the Conference met on September 30 to discuss once again the question it had hoped to avoid. Should the emperor seek a separate peace? Numerous arguments favored such a solution. Infected by disease, beset by a relentless enemy, and led by indecisive and pusillanimous officers, the army had suffered so much in the last campaign that it might experience insurmountable problems in preparing for the next one. Given the weakness of the forces, to risk another year of battle would endanger all of the gains won twenty years earlier at Passarowitz. This debility only substantial Russian help could offset, but St. Petersburg's performance in the two previous campaigns made it highly unlikely that the required assistance would be granted. Besides, the notable failure of Münnich to engage the enemy during the summer aroused strong suspicions that he and the grand vizier had already concluded a secret armistice and that a separate Russo-Turkish peace would follow shortly.[1] In that event Vienna must not only forget about Russian aid, but must rush immediately to sign a treaty before the Turks unleashed their full resources against Austria.[2] In addition to these arguments based upon the military situation, conditions in Europe generally favored an immediate settlement, for rumors circulated among the western courts that additional Habsburg defeats might tempt France, despite its mediating role, to take advantage of the Austrian discomfiture by laying claim to the long-coveted Duchy of Luxemburg.[3]

If Vienna chose to seek a separate peace, it would be easy to open negotiations with the Turks. Despite acceptance of French intercession by both sides, direct contacts remained between Ottoman and Habsburg military headquarters—Francis Stephen still possessed full power to talk directly with the enemy in the field—and between the grand vizier and Königsegg, who continued to exchange personal correspondence after the war had begun.[4] Upon receiving instructions and authorization from the emperor, either Francis Stephen or the war minister could initiate discussions at once.[5]

Only one consideration militated against the arguments for a separate peace. To reach such a settlement would alienate the Russians and thereby lead to the end of the Austro-Russian alliance and the loss of the emperor's most devoted

1 Emperor to Ostein, August 29, 1738, in HHSA, SK, Russland, II, 136.
2 Two Swedish envoys reported from Constantinople that the Russians were working feverishly toward a separate peace and sparing no expense to achieve it. Höpken and Carlson to the king of Sweden, July 6, 1738, *ibid.*
3 Braubach, *Versailles und Wien*, 311–12, 328.
4 Emperor to Lorraine, May 20, 1738, in HHSA, SK, Russland, II, 136. Münnich possessed the same powers, and both he and Lorraine promised to keep the other informed of all talks with the Turks, even though neither fully trusted the other to keep his word. Lorraine to Münnich, May 20, 1738, *ibid.*
5 Emperor to Königsegg, October 3, 1738, in *ibid.*, *Türkei*, 220.

and valuable friend. When it came time to choose between war and peace, this reason overrode all of the others; to preserve the Russian union, the Conference reluctantly but unanimously agreed that it must continue hostilities and accordingly advised Charles to prepare for another campaign.[6]

Aside from the initial determination to enter the conflict, this resolution most strongly illustrated the Austrian dependence on Russian friendship; indeed at this point the preservation of this union seemed to have become an end in itself. Whereas the original reason for preserving the accord lay in Russia's usefulness as a partner primarily in western European diplomacy, at no time during the critical discussion of September 30 did a member raise the point that perhaps the Russian friendship at that moment served no specific purpose in western European affairs. In the autumn of 1738, the Habsburg Empire was certainly not overtly threatened by any major power—France had even recognized the Pragmatic Sanction—and did not envision any serious crisis with any state in the near future. In fact, on this particular question, the Conference appeared to succumb to Bartenstein's habit of focusing attention on the immediate question without giving due consideration to the long-range impact of its decisions. Assuming therefore that the Russian alliance must be retained, the councillors chose to carry on the struggle and hope that the sacrifices would not be too great.

Having resolved to persevere, the councillors turned to the thus far unavailing task of soliciting Russian armed assistance for the coming campaign. This time believing it futile to ask St. Petersburg again to march against Khotin, Vienna requested instead that it send 20,000 troops to reinforce the Austrian army in Transylvania.[7] If Münnich persisted in

6 Konferenz Protokolle, September 30, 1738, in *ibid.*, Vorträge, 48.
7 Emperor to Ostein, August 31, 1738, in *ibid.*, Russland, II, 136.

wandering about the steppe for the fourth straight year, the Austrians reasoned, at least he could provide a few soldiers to prevent the Turks from ravishing Habsburg territory. In view of their ally's past rejections of such requests, however, they had little doubt that the empress would spurn this one as well.

Contrary to its gloomy assumptions, this time Vienna received a pleasant surprise. Even before the Austrian appeal for aid reached the Russian capital, Biron confided to Ostein that, not only did he believe Münnich would at once release 30,000 men for service in Austria, but he was certain the empress would order an advance on Khotin in order to divert the Turks from attacking Habsburg lands.[8] Just two weeks after Biron dropped these hints, Ostermann officially informed the ambassador that 20,000 well-equipped soldiers would set out for Transylvania as soon as they were fit to march.[9]

Because of St. Petersburg's past reluctance to cooperate, the councillors deemed it strange that their ally would suddenly show such deference to Austria's military needs. In truth the Russian change-of-heart had its origins in events of only indirect concern to Vienna and thus not immediately recognized or appreciated by the Habsburg policy makers. It evolved from early 1738, when the elections to the Swedish Diet produced a strong anti-Russian faction intent on reviving Swedish power in the Baltic and reconquering the lands lost to Russia in the Great Northern War. This group resolved to seek an alliance with the Ottoman Empire and force Russia into battle in both the north and the south.[10]

When the specter of a two-front war first revealed itself,

8 Ostein to emperor, September 6, 1738, in *ibid.*, 18.
9 Ostein to emperor, September 28, 1738, *ibid.*
10 Ludwig Stavenow, *Geschichte Schwedens, 1718–1772* (Gotha, 1908), 138–44.

the Russians expressed no immediate concern because they knew that Sweden lacked the resources to fight Russia without substantial financial assistance from a great European power. Later in the spring, however, as rumors reached Russia that France planned to bribe the Diet in order to create a Franco-Swedish bloc, the prospect of fighting Sweden and Turkey concurrently suddenly appeared on the brink of realization. To learn the truth behind this gossip, St. Petersburg employed every means at its disposal, from paid informants in Stockholm to Ostermann's personal communication with Cardinal Fleury.[11] But it had no success until autumn, when its worst fears were realized. From the Swedish capital came word that Sweden and France had signed a subsidy treaty by which the former promised to ally itself with no other power without permission of the latter in exchange for annual payments of 600,000 *gulden* for three years.[12] This union represented an instant danger to St. Petersburg, for it meant that at anytime within the next three years Paris could apply intense pressure on the empress by threatening to permit a Swedish-Ottoman accord and to finance an invasion of her Baltic provinces.

This Franco-Swedish pact constituted the primary reason for Russia's surprising willingness to satisfy Austria's needs. Fully aware that only Vienna enjoyed sufficient influence in Paris to keep Fleury from unleashing the Swedes, St. Petersburg had to assure the emperor of full cooperation in the forthcoming campaign, and it knew of no better way than promising to shore up its ally's forces with 20,000 Russian troops.

Just after the Russians had notified the emperor of their decision, an incident occurred between Biron and Ostein at

11 For published copies of Ostermann's correspondence with Fleury, see *Sbornik*, LXXXVI, 1–34.
12 Antivari to emperor, November 7, 1738, in HHSA, SK, Russland, II, 138.

the Russian court that briefly threatened to sabotage the newly restored amicability between the two allies. The empress' lover possessed a special status in Austro-Russian affairs because the Conference, while viewing Münnich as an outright enemy of Habsburg interests and Ostermann as a wily, untrustworthy manipulator, looked upon Biron as the only influential Russian completely devoted to Austria's interests. Warranted or not, this confidence in Biron made the association between him and Ostein the principal channel for exchanging unofficial views between the two capitals. On October 9, during a court festival, this friendship dramatically dissolved. The explosion came when Ostein, terribly agitated by Biron's mentioning that the empress expected the Austrian emperor to bear the full cost of sending the 20,000 men to Transylvania, launched into a polemic first about the enormous expense of maintaining the Russians on the Rhine in 1735, then about the sacrifices Austria had made for St. Petersburg in this conflict, and finally about the ravages the Habsburg lands had suffered, while Russia escaped unscathed. Taking these comments as insults to the Russian war effort, Biron, recalling the loss of Nish, heatedly answered that Austrian commanders were such cowards that they surrendered whole fortresses upon mere sight of the enemy. The infuriated Ostein shouted that in the whole war the Russians had killed only three Tartars, to which the empress' lover replied, if the Russians had killed only three Tartars, then the Austrians had killed only five Jews. With that, Biron stalked out of the room. A week later, when seeking to offer birthday greetings to Biron, Ostein was turned away at the door, signifying that he had become *persona non grata*.[13]

Had either side taken this exchange of insults seriously,

13 Ostein to emperor, October 22, 1738, in *ibid.*, 18.

the alliance could have been jeopardized, but, at this juncture, neither party wished any disturbance in their mutual relations. Consequently, upon hearing of Ostein's quarrel with Biron, the Conference, for some time aware of its ambassador's difficult personality, decided to replace him with Marquis Botha d'Adorno, the officer who had carried the Austrian operations plan to St. Petersburg in 1738 and had remained in the Russian capital as a military attaché.[14] More tactful, even tempered, and cooperative than Ostein, he seemed less likely to engage in needless court squabbles that would hinder his effectiveness.[15] Notwithstanding the loss of his office, Ostein stayed on in St. Petersburg as an adviser to the new envoy. For their part the Russians thanked the emperor for removing Ostein and expressed no ill-will over the clash between the two officials.

By January, 1739, the allies seemed to have reached the heights of cooperative spirit: not only had the Russians agreed to conduct their campaign along the lines proposed by the Austrians, but Vienna had vowed to employ its influence in Paris and Stockholm to prevent the Swedes from attacking Russia.[16] For the first time in this war, the two powers appeared on the verge of uniting their diplomatic policies and coordinating their military thrust for a decisive victory over the Ottomans.

No sooner had this prospect of success emerged than a new problem arose, this time in Poland. To reach Transylvania, the Russian auxiliary corps had to cross Polish territory, and,

14 Konferenz Protokolle, November 9, 1738, in *ibid.*, Vorträge, 38; emperor to empress of Russia, December 17, 1738, in *ibid.*, Russland, II, 210.

15 M. von Suhm to king of Poland, April 19, 1738, *Sbornik*, XX, 110.

16 Emperor to Lanshinsky, November 15, 1738, in HHSA, SK, Russland, II, 224; emperor to Ostein, December 8, 1738, in *ibid.*, 138. Vienna believed that Paris would never allow Sweden to conclude an accord with Turkey.

because Poland was neutral, St. Petersburg and Vienna had to secure the king's permission to do so.[17] Since they had virtually installed Augustus III on his throne and had tempted him with annexations should he take part in the war, neither the empress nor the emperor had any doubt that he would grant them the right of transit across his land. But this confidence proved unwarranted; though at first amenable, he finally refused the request and pointedly asked both sovereigns to prevent any soldier from violating the frontier.[18] The rejection by itself posed no danger to Russia, but the reasons behind it did. The king had acted out of fear of a strong confederation, formed and led by Count Potocki, primate of Poland and implacable foe of Russia, who had vowed to resist Russian encroachment on Polish soil and, if necessary, to unite with Sweden and Turkey in a collective war against Muscovite aggression.[19]

Weighing the menace of Potocki along with the threat from Sweden, the Russians reluctantly concluded that they could send no men to Austria because the empress might need every available soldier to repulse invasions from the west and north. On January 19 Ostermann called both Ostein and Botha to his home, presented them with the evidence of the strong anti-Russian faction in Poland, and informed them that the Russian reinforcements would be withheld. Anticipating the outburst of indignation he knew would erupt from

17 Empress to king of Poland, September 3/14, 1738, *ibid.*, 18. Augustus asked for the Elbgensian territory as his price for entering the war, but the emperor refused, fearing it would provoke the king of Prussia, who also had claims to that land.

18 King of Poland to empress of Russia, December 20, 1738, *ibid.*, 19.

19 Kayserling to emperor, January 22, 1739, *ibid.* A medieval Polish constitutional device, the confederation was a voluntary association of armed men who hoped to effect a specified, limited project. Confederations sometimes supported the king, sometimes opposed him, and sometimes served to prevent disorder during an interregnum.

the Habsburg court, Ostermann offered to replace the men with 1,600,000 *gulden* for use in raising and outfitting recruits in Germany.[20]

The Conference quite naturally felt greatly distressed by this change of mind and by the offer of money, and immediately informed St. Petersburg of its disappointment, adding that it felt the Russians exaggerated the Swedish-Polish threat and should send the troops anyway.[21] Before receiving this expression of dismay, however, the Russians informed Vienna that, because they could not send a reinforcing corps to Transylvania, they would satisfy a long-sought Habsburg desire by investing Khotin regardless of the consequences of violating Polish neutrality. Whereas the Polish dissidents might harass a Russian corps of 20,000 men, the Russians added, they would never dare challenge the major Russian army, and therefore the crossing of Polish land should present no difficulties. Although informed of this decision on March 11, Botha, understandably skeptical, refused to notify Vienna until two days later when, at a dinner party given for all the resident foreign envoys, Münnich confirmed its truth.[22] On March 20, the empress officially advised the emperor that this year her soldiers' primary objective would be the conquest of Khotin.[23]

Endeavoring to display even more obviously Russia's good will toward its ally, Empress Anne announced the marriage of her niece and only offspring of the senior branch of the Romanov family to the nephew of the Habsburg empress, Anthony Ulrich Brunswick-Bevern-Luneburg. Although un-

20 Botha and Ostein to emperor, January 22, 1739, in HHSA, SK, Russland, II, 19. Irritated but not surprised by what he considered Russian bad faith, Ostein asked why Ostermann, who had paid no attention to the Polish magnates earlier, should worry about them now.
21 Emperor to Botha and Hohenholz, March 9, 1739, *ibid.*, 139.
22 Botha to emperor, March 14, 1739, *ibid.*, 19.
23 Empress to emperor, March 20, 1739, *ibid.*

der consideration for some time before 1739, this union had not received official approval at the Russian court largely because Biron had dreams of matching the empress' niece with his own son in order to give his family a claim to the Russian throne. Now the diplomatic situation required an overt gesture of friendship for Austria and, notwithstanding the Courland lover's disappointment, this marriage sufficed. After making the formal declaration, Anne remarked to the imperial ambassador that she wished to celebrate this wedding with the greatest pomp possible, in order to show all the world the "eternal alliance" between the houses of Romanov and Habsburg.[24]

All of these protestations of friendship the councillors gratefully accepted, but they did not fully appreciate the Russian motives. In direct contrast to St. Petersburg's interpretation, the Habsburg advisers looked upon the Franco-Swedish accord not as intensifying the threat of a Swedish attack on Russia, but diminishing it. Because they accepted at face value the cardinal's repeated statements that Sweden had not signed, nor had even begun negotiations regarding, an alliance with the Ottomans, the Conference believed that Fleury would curtail, not stimulate, Stockholm's ambitions in the Baltic. Passing these assurances on to St. Petersburg, the councillors informed the empress that she need not worry about events in the north and by no means should pull any troops out of the Ukraine for service on the Baltic coast.[25]

Regardless of the emperor's efforts to play down the Franco-Swedish danger, the Russian policy makers remained con-

24 Botha to emperor, *ibid.* This union produced Anne's successor, Ivan VI, born August, 1740. At the tender age of three months he became Tsar, only to be removed by Empress Elizabeth in 1741. For details of the family, see A. Brückner, *Die Familie Braunschweig im achtzehnten Jahrhundert* (St. Petersburg, 1876).

25 Liechtenstein to emperor, January 18, 1739, in HHSA, SK, Russland, II, 138; emperor to Botha, April 11, 1739, *ibid.*, 139.

cerned, and rightly so, for in April Fleury added Prussia to his northern system by guaranteeing Berlin a portion of the duchy of Berg.[26] Shortly thereafter five French men-of-war entered the Baltic, ostensibly bound for the Gulf of Bothnia but possibly to be used to protect Swedish amphibious operations against Russia.[27] At the same time, the Swedish Diet, which had remained in session well past its scheduled adjournment, sent 2,000 soldiers to Finland to erect a new fortress— and possible staging point—on the Russian frontier.[28]

In the midst of all this activity, an incident occurred which threatened to plunge Russia and Sweden immediately into war. It involved a mysterious Major Sinclair, a Swedish officer who traveled regularly between Stockholm and Constantinople and who, St. Petersburg feared, carried the correspondence regarding a secret Turko-Swedish alliance.[29] On June 17, just before Sinclair crossed from Silesia to Saxony on one of his journeys, a troop of Russian cavalry stopped his coach, forced him to step down, took him into a nearby forest, seized his satchel supposedly containing the final draft of the agreement, killed him, and rode off.[30]

Sinclair's murder caused a sensation throughout the capitals of Europe. At the Habsburg and Romanov courts, the French, British, and Dutch envoys expressed official horror

26 Droysen, *Geschichte der preussischen Politik*, IV, Pt. 4, 473– 77; Wilson, *French Foreign Policy*, 318. The British also disliked the treaty because they feared France's growing influence on the continent. Vaucher, *Robert Walpole et la politique de Fleury*, 224.

27 Botha to Liechtenstein, May 7, 1739, in HHSA, SK, Russland, II, 19. The French squadron might have been a response to a Russian fleet of 7 warships and 100 galleys, which set sail from St. Petersburg in April. Botha to Sinzendorf, April 21, 1739, *ibid.*

28 Botha to emperor, June 9, 1739, *ibid.*

29 Walter to Brühl, July 8, 1738, *Sbornik*, XX, 125. The Russian ambassador in Stockholm told the Polish ambassador that his king would render the empress a great service if he had Sinclair kidnapped and blamed his disappearance on bandits.

30 Statement of Jean André Couturrier (a merchant riding with Sinclair), *Sbornik*, XX, 132–34.

at such a villainous act, and the Swedish ministers threatened Russia with an instant declaration of war. In reply the two monarchs both expressed strong disapproval of the deed and claimed complete ignorance about the affair. The emperor promised to do all that he could to prevent an outbreak of the fighting in the north, and the empress vowed to bring the culprits to justice.[31] Behind this public display of joint innocence, Vienna, apparently convinced that the Russians had specifically ordered the deed, admonished St. Petersburg for the assassination, emphasizing that Sinclair probably carried no treaty (which indeed he did not) and decrying the act as a flirtation with a two-front war.[32] Ostermann personally responded by denying any foreknowledge of the plot and pledging to find and punish those responsible.[33] Undoubtedly the foreign minister's disavowal of guilt was sincere because he knew that such a provocative act would spark the very conflict he hoped to avoid.

St. Petersburg's concern over the Franco-Swedish menace was of essential importance because it finally persuaded the Russians, especially Ostermann, to abandon their dreams of expansion and seek a settlement with minimal annexations. Having already lost Ochakov and Kinburn to the plague, they hoped at first to retain Azov, the last remnant of the lands won and lost by Peter the Great; but realizing by April that the need for peace outweighed the need for Azov, they sent word

31 Emperor to Botha and Hohenholz, July 17, 1739, in HHSA, SK, Russland, II, 140. Many contemporaries believed that Münnich was responsible for ordering the murder, although a commission created to investigate his complicity found no incriminating evidence. Brühl to Walter and Brais, June 22, 1739, *Sbornik*, XX, 135; Botha to emperor, July 19, 1739, in HHSA, SK, Russland, II, 20; Christian Friedrich Hempel, *Leben, Thaten, und berümbter Fall des weltberufenen russischen Grafen Burchards Christophs von Münnich* (Bremen, 1743), 451.

32 Emperor to Botha and Hohenholz, July 17, 1739, in HHSA, SK, Russland, II, 140.

33 Botha to emperor, July 19, 1739, *ibid.*, 20.

through Ostermann to Villeneuve that they would be willing to give back that critical fortress to the Ottomans and settle for only minor rectifications.[34] To carry this implied admission of defeat, Ostermann appointed a Florentine adventurer named Cagnoni, whom he also empowered to accompany the French mediator and protect Russian interests in the talks with the Turks.[35]

This novel Russian desire to end the war without acquisitions of course corresponded with the long-standing Austrian objective to do the same. By the time St. Petersburg realized the need for peace, however, Vienna had become absolutely desperate. As Starhemberg warned the Council in January, 1739: "The condition of things is as bad as could be. The crownlands are desolate, the treasury deep in debt. One can do nothing against the Turks. If one battle is lost, everything is lost. It would be a stroke of good luck to make peace by any means. In another campaign Austria could win nothing, but might lose everything." [36] Whereas St. Petersburg was willing to foresake its recently won gains for a settlement, Vienna now was happy to sacrifice some of its own territory. Accordingly in early March the Conference notified Villeneuve that it would give Austrian Serbia and Wallachia to the sultan if he would return the fortresses of New Orsova and Mehadia.[37] Such a solution would leave Belgrade as the emperor's only possession on the right bank of the Danube.

With Austria and Russia convinced of the necessity of ending the struggle, only the Ottoman Empire appeared ready to continue, but by the spring of 1739, its bellicosity had declined as well. Oppressed by heavy taxation, a simmering re-

---

34 Vandal, *Une ambassade française*, 332–33.
35 Uebersberger, *Russlands Orientpolitik*, 226–27.
36 Konferenz Protokolle, January 19, 1739, in HHSA, SK, Vorträge, 48.
37 Sinzendorf to Villeneuve, March 11, 1739, in *ibid.*, Türkei, 220.

volt in Asia, and dwindling food supplies, Constantinople had lost much of the enthusiasm generated by the earlier military advances and the inspired leadership of Jegen Mohammed.[38] Over the winter a powerful peace party, led by the prestigious Kizlar Aga, had emerged to challenge the arrogant and self-righteous grand vizier and to demand that the conflict come to an immediate close.[39]

Although it achieved little success at first, this faction gained decisive influence when, in March, the khan of the Crimean Tartars appeared in Constantinople, on behalf of his terribly devastated land, to beg the sultan for peace and freedom from the annual Russian raids.[40] Swayed by the emotional pleas of the khan and the advice of the Kizlar Aga, the sultan removed Jegen Mohammed and replaced him with the pasha of Vidin, a strong member of the peace party.[41] One month later this new grand vizier held an audience with Villeneuve to discuss the procedure for beginning talks, and on May 19 the Sultan with great ceremony invested the Frenchman with the power to conclude a treaty on behalf of the Turks.[42]

By April, 1739, all belligerents wanted peace, but to translate this desire into reality—to coordinate proposals, arrange meetings, and conduct negotiations—required time, too much time to prevent one more campaign. Consequently, as preparations for the forthcoming talks began, the three antagonists set out to fight one last summer of battle, a summer each hoped would yield final victory.

38 Cassels, *The Struggle for the Ottoman Empire*, 160.
39 Emperor to Antivari, January 31, 1739, in HHSA, SK, Russland, II, 138.
40 Uebersberger, *Russlands Orientpolitik*, 225–26.
41 Hammer, *Geschichte des osmanischen Reiches*, VII, 524.
42 Villeneuve to Sinzendorf, April 30, 1739, in HHSA, SK, Russland, II, 139. For details of the investiture see Vandal, *Une ambassade française*, 360–67.

VIII

❧ Last Campaign and
Unfortunate Treaty

Faced with the inevitability of a third campaign,
Vienna once again tackled the unrewarding task of selecting
a commander in chief, one who would hopefully reverse the
misfortunes of 1737 and 1738. This time the emperor chose
Field Marshal Count Oliver Wallis, a 65-year old Irishman
with forty years of service under the imperial flag. Haughty,
obstinate, overbearing, and intolerant of criticism, Wallis
tried to hide his deficiencies behind a mask of formality and
secrecy. An inveterate pessimist, he emphasized the hopeless-
ness of every military situation in order to absolve himself of
guilt in case of defeat. Frederick the Great wrote that, upon
learning of his appointment, Wallis commented: " 'The Emperor has made me commander of his army: The first who led
it is in prison; the second has become a eunuch of the palace;
the only thing left for me is to have my head cut off at the
conclusion of the campaign.' " [1] Whether a genuine utterance
or a figment of Frederick's imagination, the pessimism reflected in this quote certainly pervaded the field marshal's de-

1 Frederick the Great, *Mémoires pour servir à l'histoire de la
maison de Brandebourg* (Berlin, 1846), 172.

cisions in 1739. To strike with confidence and good judgment seemed foreign to his personality.

Despite his shortcomings Wallis enjoyed important advantages over his predecessors. Acquiring the right to veto all decisions of his generals and to formulate strategy without referring to Vienna, he had to follow no prearranged military plan. In April, 1739, three meetings of high-ranking officers took place in the *Hofkriegsrat* to determine operations; but Wallis objected so vehemently to all suggestions that the others assumed he had formulated his own battle scheme and simply chose not to reveal it. Hoping that the field marshal's hidden plan would yield a decisive victory, the *Hofkriegsrat* elected to issue no restrictive orders to him but to allow him to proceed on his own initiative.[2] In addition to this freedom of command, Wallis had the good fortune of facing far fewer Turks than had the two previous leaders, owing to the Russian penetration of Moldavia. Knowing that the enemy's strength in Serbia had diminished, therefore, he could seek a climactic encounter with an excellent chance of emerging victorious. The final benefit held by Wallis was his power to make peace in the field. Both Seckendorf and Francis Stephen had held such authority, but, because in 1739 there appeared little doubt that Vienna wanted a settlement at the end of the campaign regardless of battlefield developments, this prerogative assumed much greater importance in Wallis' case.

The situation demanded a commander with courage and aggressiveness, but unfortunately Wallis possessed neither. Even though he enjoyed complete freedom of action, he refused to act on his own initiative. After he joined his troops in mid-April on the frontier, he advised Vienna that the army would not begin fighting until his staff received detailed instructions from the *Hofkriegsrat*. In this dispatch he sug-

2 Brown "Türkenkrieg," 1739, pp. 91–93.

gested that the men cross the Danube and seek the enemy's main force in Serbia, but emphasized that not one company would decamp until he had received a direct command from the capital.[3] Surprised by the field marshal's request, the *Hofkriegsrat* quickly authorized his recommendations, composed the proper orders, and directed him to march immediately.[4] Nevertheless a petty dispute between the commander and one of his subordinates delayed the beginning of operations until early July.[5]

In 1739 the army, reinforced by recruits from the crownlands and by regulars on loan from various European states, numbered more than 45,000, a force equal to those of 1737 and 1738.[6] The main body under Wallis' command contained slightly more than 30,000, while an auxiliary corps, led by Count Reinhard William Neipperg, made up the balance.[7] The immediate enemy of these soldiers seemed to be not the Turks but the plague, which still ravaged the Danubian floodland. Nonetheless the Austrians hoped to crush the Turks before illness seriously depleted the ranks.[8]

By mid-July Wallis' command had reached Belgrade, where it encamped to await the arrival of Neipperg's units coming from Timişoara. While resting Wallis learned that his reconnaissance patrols had sighted the grand vizier's army

3 *Ibid.*, 111–25.
4 *Ibid.*, 133–44.
5 The dispute involved Wallis and General Reinhard William Neipperg, who argued that he lacked the necessary men to fulfill Wallis' orders to cover the Turks at Orsova while the main army marched south to engage the Turks at Nish. Even though the Turks negated both officers' arguments by marching toward Belgrade and forcing the Austrians onto the defensive, much ill feeling continued between the two throughout this year's campaign. *Ibid.*, 160–86.
6 Details of the European contributions in men to the Habsburg war effort can be found in *ibid.*, Appendix D.
7 *Ibid.*, Appendix DD, EE.
8 Threat of the plague constituted the official reason for Francis Stephen's failure to participate in this campaign. *Ibid.*, 91.

near Smederevo, a few miles east of Belgrade, and that a large company of Turks had taken up positions near the village of Grocka, six hours' march southeast of the imperial camp.[9] Realizing that the grand vizier's full army would follow close behind this force, Wallis convened a war council of his senior officers to decide whether the army should advance immediately on Grocka to dislodge this forward Ottoman unit or to wait for Neipperg's 15,000, about a day's march behind the main army, and then move up with all the available Austrian manpower to engage the enemy. The council concluded that the cavalry should go on ahead to remove the Turks from Grocka, then the infantry should follow close behind and take up defensive positions around the village. Even if the Turks attacked these lines in the next day or two, Neipperg's corps would reinforce the main contingent within twenty-four hours, and thus the whole Austrian army would be assembled to give battle to the oncoming Turks.[10] Consequently at 10:00 P.M. on July 21, the cavalry, accompanied by Wallis, left camp for Grocka.[11]

Winding through low hills and lovely vineyards, the road that the Austrians traversed paralleled, but did not border, the Danube. Just before reaching Grocka, it gently ascended to a narrow defile scarcely wide enough for a carriage, then descended to two open hills planted with vineyards. In front of the hills, the road broke to the left, then back to the right, and passed through the village resting on the riverbank.

Unbeknown to imperial headquarters, during the night of July 21 the grand vizier, sensing Wallis' intention, had moved his whole army to Grocka to support his advance units. By morning the Turks had constructed their defenses on the two

9 *Ibid.*, 221. The sighting was reported on July 21 by the commander of the Danubian war fleet.
10 *Ibid.*, 223.
11 *Ibid.*, 228.

hills, so that they could concentrate their fire on the narrow pass and the road running below them.

As the Austrian forces approached Grocka, the advance squadrons of cavalry, eager to engage the enemy, outran the foot soldiers to the rear and reached the defile well ahead of the rest of the troops. At dawn on July 22, when the cavalry burst through the narrow pass, the Turks commenced a murderous fire which broke the charge and forced the horsemen to dismount. Unable to press the attack because of the violent fusilade and the difficult terrain, the troops formed into small units to prevent the Turks from closing the defile behind them. Despite heavy losses the cavalry stood its ground until midmorning, when forward companies of grenadiers came to their rescue and stabilized the ranks.[12]

Notwithstanding the arrival of the foot soldiers, the imperial position had become extremely precarious. Taking advantage of the Austrian concentration on the road, the grand vizier had ordered some units to advance to the ridge on either side of the defile, which, if occupied, would allow them to surround the cavalry and grenadiers and to inflict heavy damage on the infantry and artillery advancing up the highway. Sensing the danger Hildburghausen, the officer commanding the line troops, ordered his men to leave the road, occupy the heights protecting the pass, and force the enemy elements to withdraw. These soldiers succeeded and, after forming into battle order along the heights, poured their fire into the Ottoman positions on the hills. Under the protective cover of the imperial guns, the cavalry remnant withdrew, leaving the grenadiers to carry on the struggle at the Turkish front.[13]

12 Eighteen companies of grenadiers, partly Austrian and partly Bavarian, formed the advance guard that relieved the cavalry. Wrede, *Geschichte der k. und k. Wehrmacht*, II, 227.

13 Brown, "Türkenkrieg," 1739, pp. 238–47. For published accounts of the battle, see Angeli, "Der Krieg mit der Pforte," 454–56;

The battle raged all day long, with both sides exchanging torrents of metal and suffering heavy losses. Only at nightfall did the action subside, when the Turks fell back leaving the Habsburg forces in command of the field. The Austrian casualties attest to the severity of the struggle: the dead numbered 2,222 and wounded 2,942, including 10 generals.[14] Whole squadrons of cavalry died, including half the officers and men of the Count Palffy Curaissiers, the first unit to engage the enemy.[15] Even a year after the encounter, evidence of its violence impressed a passing traveler, Francis Gudenus, who described the scene "Today one cannot go ten steps without stepping on human corpses piled on top of another, all only half decomposed, many still in uniforms. Lying about are maimed bodies, hats, saddles, cartridge belts, boots, cleaning utensils, drumcases, and other cavalry equipment. Everything is embedded in underbrush. In the surrounding countryside, peasants use skulls as scarecrows; many wear hats, and one even wears a wig." [16]

Technically the Austrians won, for they occupied the enemy's positions at nightfall. Not only had they emerged victorious, but it appeared that, with the arrival of Neipperg's fresh 15,000 after sundown, they could pursue the Turks even farther down the Danube in the morning. Neipperg and Hildburghausen particularly encouraged Wallis to adopt this

and Keralio, *Histoire de la guerre*, II, 152–64. The Austrians reported that in this battle some Turkish units practiced European tactics for the first time; when their lines broke, they fell back and regrouped, rather than flee headlong from the field of battle as they had in the past. Some units wielded bayonets, never before used by the Ottomans. Many Europeans attributed these innovations to Bonneval. Benedikt, *Alexander von Bonneval*, 130.

14 Brown, "Türkenkrieg," 1739, Appendix KK.

15 Of the 931 men in this regiment, 364 were killed and 103 wounded. *Ibid.*

16 Gerhard Fritsch, *Paschas und Pest* (Graz and Vienna, 1962), 58, 60.

strategy; one more battle, they argued, would yield a victory equal to those of the mighty Prince Eugene.[17] At this juncture, when the fortunes of war at last appeared to favor the emperor, the commander in chief ordered a general retreat. Accompanying the cavalry in the thick of the fighting, the field marshal had lost what little aggressiveness he had. Oppressed by the carnage and discouraged by the formidable resistance of the Turks, he ignored the advice of his officers and issued the command to withdraw to Belgrade.

Unfortunately, even after arriving at Belgrade, the army could not rest because on the left bank of the Danube, another Turkish force of 16,000 had gathered, hoping to harrass the imperial supply lines in the Banat. To nullify this threat, Wallis led his men across the river and, near the fortress of Pančevo, attacked the Turks and forced them to flee.[18]

This engagement, fought on July 30, marked the second Austrian success in eight days. Had Wallis taken advantage of either one, he could have substantially strengthened his military posture. By pursuing his victory at Grocka, he could have pushed the Turks deep into Serbia; by pressing his advantage at Pančevo, he could have erased the Ottoman threat to the Banat and ended any menace to Belgrade. But Wallis did neither: in fact, he worsened his situation markedly. Believing after Pančevo that it would be too risky to recross the Danube near Belgrade, he marched his men thirty miles up the left bank of the Tisa River, found a safe place to pass over to the right bank, and marched them the same thirty miles down to Borsha, a fortified point across the Danube from Belgrade.[19] By August 11, when the army reached Borsha, the regulars were exhausted, the officers disgruntled—and the Turks were encamped before Belgrade.

17 Brown, "Türkenkrieg," 1739, p. 226.
18 *Ibid.*, 265–74.
19 Angeli, "Der Krieg mit der Pforte," 461.

For the third consecutive year, the Habsburg capital received news of Austrian victories followed by Austrian retreat. Almost at a loss as to how to react to this misfortune, the Conference decided to censure Wallis, but to leave him in command in order not to undermine the confidence of the men in their superiors. Nonetheless, now having painfully realized their commander in chief's pessimism and timidity, the councillors agreed that he must be stripped of his peacemaking powers. In a moment of weakness, they feared, he might give away much Austrian territory—possibly mighty Belgrade itself—without the emperor's approval.[20]

To assume the role of chief negotiator in Wallis' place, Vienna picked his subordinate, Count Neipperg. A descendent of a Swabian knightly family with a long tradition of Habsburg service, Neipperg had entered the imperial army as one of the many protégés of Prince Eugene. A veteran of dealings with the Turks, in 1718 he had led the imperial delegation to establish permanent boundaries between the Ottoman and Austrian empires.[21] In 1723 he received the distinguished appointment of tutor to Francis Stephen of Lorraine and by 1726 had won regard as "one of the most knowledgeable officers in the imperial command."[22]

Neipperg's appointment assumed immediate significance, for the Conference had formally agreed that a settlement must be reached at the end of this campaign. Wallis' withdrawal,

20 Konferenz Protokolle, July 31, 1739, in HHSA, SK, Vorträge, 49.
21 Oddly enough, on July 26 Wallis informed the *Hofkriegsrat* that he proposed to employ Neipperg as his intermediary in his dealings with the grand vizier because of the general's experience in Turkish affairs. Brown, "Türkenkrieg," 1739, p. 555.
22 Oskar Regele, "Die Schuld des Grafen Reinhard Wilhelm von Neippergs am Belgrader Frieden, 1739, und an der Niederlage von Mollwitz, 1741," *Mitteilungen des österreichischen Staatsarchivs*, VII (1954), 374. Neipperg was the grandfather of the second husband of the French empress, Marie Louise (Napoleon's second wife) and the great-grandfather of the first Prince Montenuovo.

no reports of progress from Russian headquarters, and news of the Turkish investment of Belgrade convinced the Habsburg ministers of the impossibility of future success and the very real possibility of serious misfortune. As Bartenstein informed Charles: "If Belgrade is lost, all of southern Hungary will be open to the Turks, and the army would be unable to eject them in 1740." [23] Even before Neipperg's selection, this bleak opinion had prompted Bartenstein—in the name of the emperor—to inform Villeneuve that Vienna would gladly surrender New Orsova if it could keep Timişoara and Belgrade. He even informed the French envoy that he would assume the responsibility of ceding Azov to the Porte without Russian official consent.[24] Such willingness to incur the wrath of the Russians amply displayed the earnestness of the emperor's advisers' desire for peace.

Austria's fate would ultimately lie in the hands of Neipperg himself, for he would be responsible for conducting the negotiations in the inhospitable atmosphere of the grand vizier's camp. There he would deal with not only the Turks, but with the Russian representative, Cagnoni, and Villeneuve, both of whom had taken up residence in the camp in preparation for the talks. On August 10 the Conference undertook the weighty task of composing the instructions for Neipperg to follow. Because distance prevented the count from referring frequently to Vienna, the ministers had to provide him with alternative solutions to cover various contingencies. After long and heated debate, the Conference concluded that, if the field army remained near Belgrade and could prevent the Turks from taking the fortress, Neipperg should offer no terms other than those relayed by Bartenstein to Villeneuve. Should Belgrade appear likely to fall, Neipperg would agree to destroy

---

23 Bartenstein to emperor, August 10, 1739, in HHSA, SK, Vorträge, 49.
24 Emperor to Wallis, August 8, 1739, in *ibid.*, Türkei, 220.

its fortifications, in exchange for a Turkish promise to level the walls of New Orsova. Finally, if the surrender of Belgrade seemed inevitable, Neipperg should consent "to allow the Turks to possess Belgrade with its walls intact, so that the Danube and the Sava become the borders; everything which lies in the Banat, including Mehadia and Old Orsova, would remain to me [the emperor]." [25]

Such instructions depended, of course, on Neipperg having a thorough understanding of the military situation, thus, the Conference advised him to inspect the field army and the garrison of Belgrade before departing for the Turkish camp to begin negotiations. After warning the plenipotentiary to beware of Wallis' pessimistic accounts and to take care to examine the "true status" of affairs, the emperor emphasized that, while on his inspection tour and at the grand vizier's headquarters, the count should keep Vienna fully informed of all developments. [26] These orders placed great responsibility on Neipperg, not only as a minister, but as a military analyst as well, for much depended upon his ability to assess the strategic posture correctly. The command to remain in contact with the court constituted the only check on his authority.

Having sent Neipperg off to examine the army and then to enter the Ottoman war camp, the Habsburg government turned its attention again to events in the field. By the third week of August, despair had wholly gripped Wallis, who,

25 Emperor to Neipperg, August 11, 1739, *ibid.;* Konferenz Protokolle, August 19, 1739, in *ibid.*, Vorträge, 49. For a discussion of these instructions, see Regele, "Schuld des Grafen Neippergs," 377–78.

26 Emperor to Neipperg, August 11, 1739, in HHSA, SK, Türkei, 220. In a secret letter written to Neipperg at the insistence of the emperor, Francis Stephen warned the general not to show his instructions to Wallis and not to trust his judgment because "the Field Marshal depicts the state of the army as one intimidated and discouraged, totally unable to view the enemy without fear of being defeated." Brown, "Türkenkrieg," 1739, pp. 374–75.

after reiterating the hopeless condition of his men, implored the emperor to abandon Belgrade and conclude an immediate peace.[27] When he had sent this dispatch, he moved the army from its camp near the threatened fortress to more secure positions up the Danube.[28] By this time most suspicious of the commander in chief's reports, the councillors decided not to accept his accounts at face value but to send another officer to headquarters to conduct a special investigation of conditions at the front. To perform this task Charles chose General Schmettau, the Protestant officer who had suffered disgrace with Seckendorf in 1737. When he left for southern Hungary, Schmettau carried with him orders not only to examine the military situation, but also to command Wallis to cease falling back and to return to Belgrade.[29] Upon receiving these instructions, Wallis protested vigorously that he could not follow them, but, after listening to Schmettau's arguments in their favor, agreed to reverse his strategy and prepare to engage the Turks. Notwithstanding his compliance the field marshal felt personally insulted by this forced change of plans and, as a token of revenge, he appointed Schmettau commander of Belgrade, replacing General Succow, one of Bartenstein's close friends.[30]

Schmettau's appointment proved a blessing in disguise.

27 Brown, "Türkenkrieg," 1739, pp. 367–556.
28 Schmettau believed that the loss of his peace-making powers so enraged Wallis that he pulled his army away from Belgrade, hoping that it would fall. Schmettau, *Mémoires secrets*, 231.
29 Brown, "Türkenkrieg," 1739, pp. 358–60.
30 The *Hofkriegsrat* had not authorized the replacement of Succow by Schmettau, and in fact on September 3, before hearing of the conclusion of the peace treaty, ordered Succow reinstated as commanding officer. Wallis' original reason for excusing Succow was his health, for the Belgrade commander had suffered from recurring bouts of fever throughout the campaign. Apparently quite ill from these attacks, Succow found it necessary to leave the front even before he received the letter reappointing him commander of Belgrade. *Ibid.*, 456–57.

Upon arriving at his new command, he found the garrison in surprisingly good condition—numbering 11,390 able soldiers —and concluded that the fortress' only weakness lay in his predecessor's preparations for defense. By redistributing the men and utilizing all of the available artillery, the new commander improved both the ability of the fortress to resist and the morale of the troops.[31] On August 29 a raiding party under his personal leadership staged a successful assault on the Borsha redoubt, a fortification directly across the Danube that had fallen to the Turks after Wallis' retreat; and, inspired by this victory, on August 30 his chief officers began formulating plans for repeating Prince Eugene's astounding attack on the Turkish camp outside Belgrade.[32] Upon hearing of the reconquest of the Borsha redoubt and the evolving plans for a decisive engagement with the main Turkish army, Wallis regained some of his nerve and sent out the command to speed the field army's return to Belgrade.[33]

Accompanying the news of Schmettau's successes and Wallis' new-found courage, word reached Vienna that Münnich was about to cross the Dniester and besiege Khotin.[34] Buoyed by these optimistic reports, the Conference took heart that conditions had substantially improved since early August and agreed that, God willing, Schmettau and Wallis would rout the Turks before Belgrade, Münnich would conquer Khotin, and the allies could at last impose an advantageous peace upon the Turks. As a reflection of this brightening outlook, the emperor ordered Neipperg, who had left for the

31 Schmettau to Wallis, August 27, 1739, *ibid.*, 412–18, Appendix TTT.

32 Angeli, "Der Krieg mit der Pforte," 247–50.

33 *Ibid.*, 252. On September 23, 1739, the *Hofkriegsrat* issued a direct order to Wallis to return the field army to the vicinity of Belgrade, and undoubtedly this command had some influence on Wallis' decision to move. Brown, "Türkenkrieg," 1739, p. 364.

34 Reysky to Harrach, August 15, 1739, in HHSA, Reichskanzlei, Russland, 33.

Turkish camp on August 17, to continue to follow his instructions of August 11, but not to present the *optimum pessimum* clause ceding Belgrade to the Ottoman Empire.[35] Curiously, however, at the time the emperor dispatched this revision, Vienna had received no notice of Neipperg; in fact, it did not even know if he had arrived in the enemy camp safely. Although finding this situation unusual, the Conference did not regard it alarming, for, as a plenipotentiary, the count enjoyed the protection of Villeneuve, who assumed responsibility for the safety of his person and the inviolability of his correspondence.[36]

On September 3 the Conference finally chose to recall Neipperg and to remove his authority to make peace. It did so not because it feared he was in danger or disapproved of his conduct, but because the situation had changed so markedly that his instructions no longer applied. Trusting that soon the allies would effect great military victories, the councillors believed that a settlement more to their satisfaction could be reached at another formal peace congress rather than through substitute diplomats in the war camp of the grand vizier.[37]

Then into the midst of this new confidence came shattering news. On September 7 General Mercy d'Argenteau arrived in Vienna after an exhausting ride from southern Hungary to inform Charles that Neipperg had formally turned over mighty Belgrade and all of Serbia to the Turks.[38] The emperor, the government, and the city were thunderstruck. "The reading and examination of these preliminaries threw everyone into dismay. The shock at the conclusion of them reverberated through the whole city of Vienna. One saw faces drawn by a profound sadness and indignation. One heard

35 Emperor to Neipperg, August 31, 1739, in *ibid.*, SK, Türkei, 220.
36 Emperor to Neipperg, September 5, 1739, *ibid.*
37 Conference Protocol, September 3, 1739, in *ibid.*, Vorträge, 49.
38 Neipperg to emperor, September 2, 1739, in *ibid.*, Türkei, 219.

bitter sighs and threats reiterated a thousand times against the Grand Vizier and the ambassador of France [Villeneuve]." [39] At the court the papal nuncio, convinced that French intrigue had precipitated the debacle, raged at the French envoy: "The Marquis de Villeneuve has sacrificed to the Turks and to his master the welfare of Christianity, the interests of the Empire, and the honor of the Emperor." [40]

Why did Neipperg consent to such an unfortunate peace? What had happened in the camp of the Grand Vizier? The answers to both these questions stem from the period preceding the general's reception of his peace-making powers. Neipperg had arrived at Grocka on the evening following the battle enthusiastic about pursuing the Turks, but he had become deeply discouraged by Wallis' decision to retreat, a decision he felt ruined all chances for future success. [41] From then on the general's depression increased until it had seriously crippled his ability to view conditions objectively. When inspecting the army before entering the Turkish encampment, for example, his pessimism drew him to the conclusion that the Habsburg field forces were far weaker than they actually were, and that the Belgrade garrison, already under heavy attack, could rely on only minimal assistance from the main units and could resist only a few weeks longer. [42]

When the Austrian plenipotentiary reached the grand vizier's headquarters on August 18, his mood scarcely improved. He found, to his complete surprise, that since late July Wallis had exchanged proposals with the Turks through an executive officer, Colonel Anthony Charles Gross who, the Ottomans asserted, had offered to surrender Belgrade in the

39 La Lande, *Histoire de L'empereur Charles VI*, V, 139.
40 *Ibid.*, 138.
41 Brown, "Türkenkrieg," 1739, p. 227.
42 Neipperg to Francis Stephen of Lorraine, August 16, 1739, *ibid.*, 375–76. See also Appendix VVV.

field marshal's own name.[43] Whether or not the colonel had made such a statement was of little importance because Neipperg discovered that his hosts refused to talk of anything except the acquisition of Belgrade. Disturbed by the unwillingness of the Turks to discuss a compromise, the general requested permission to leave camp immediately for further instructions. To his astonishment the grand vizier refused, even threatening him with punishment for spying if he delayed negotiations any longer. At this point Neipperg sought and received protection and solace in the tent of the mediator Villeneuve.[44] Even though his person was secure, he now had to face the formidable negotiating skill of the grand vizier who, sensing his overwhelming psychological advantage, never overlooked an opportunity to impress upon the count the huge number of men in his army—150,000 in camp and 25,000 on the left bank of the Danube—all of whom burned with desire to storm Belgrade and none of whom would return home without witnessing its surrender. Day after day the Turkish officials insisted that peace depended upon its

43 On July 26, at the grand vizier's request, Wallis sent Colonel Gross and a Captain Schulenberg to the Turkish camp to discuss peace terms. According to Gross's report, the grand vizier tried to bully him into persuading Wallis to cede Belgrade by saying that Hungary and Transylvania were on the verge of rebellion against the Habsburgs, and that the cost of surrendering Belgrade would be cheap compared to what Vienna would lose in case of revolutions in these two lands. Gross replied that he knew no trouble existed in either province, that the army would defend Belgrade vigorously, and that no terms should be discussed until the arrival of the French mediator, Villeneuve, who was not yet present in the Ottoman camp. *Ibid.*, Appendix RR. In his defense Neipperg related that, while on a second visit to the grand vizier's camp on August 14, Gross promised to cede Belgrade to the Turks in Wallis' name. No evidence of such a promise exists, however, therefore perhaps the Ottoman negotiators were trying to bluff Neipperg. *Ibid.*, Appendix 40; see also Regele, "Die Schuld des Grafen Neippergs," 377.

44 Neipperg to Wallis and Succow, August 28, 1739, in Brown, "Turkenkrieg," 1739, Appendix EEEE.

occupation, and day after day the Austrian's despair increased.

Vienna's late August reports about the improved condition of the army and the instructions not to sacrifice Belgrade should have greatly improved Neipperg's mood, but indeed they did not, for he never received these messages. Upon passing through the Austrian lines, Neipperg had warned Wallis to use care in sending him letters because the Turks might read them or refuse to deliver them. The field marshal, still resenting the transfer of his peace-making powers to Neipperg, complied willingly and refused to allow any correspondence whatsoever to reach him, even letters from the emperor himself.[45] Consequently no new information came to the plenipotentiary's attention, and he continued to act upon his instructions of August 11 and his observations of August 16 and 17, unaware that neither applied any longer.

For fourteen days Neipperg toiled, presenting each of the steps in his outline and hearing each rejected by the Turks until he finally came to the last. At the decisive meeting on August 29, he offered to surrender Belgrade, if the Austrians could destroy the fortifications built since 1718 and financed by the Roman Catholic Church. The grand vizier accepted these terms, but he insisted that Turkish units occupy the gates immediately and the imperial soldiers begin leveling the

45 *Ibid.* Despite his loss of peace-making powers, Wallis continued to correspond with the grand vizier and Vienna concerning peace terms and persisted in recommending to both the cession of Belgrade to the Turks and the adoption of the Danube-Sava River line as the Ottoman-Habsburg boundary. Twice the *Hofkriegsrat* ordered Wallis to stop interfering, and on August 23 expressly ordered him not to communicate with Neipperg because the Turks might open the letters and assume Wallis' suggestions to correspond to official Habsburg policy. *Ibid.*, 277–83, On August 29 Wallis reported that he had received instructions for Neipperg from the *Hofkriegsrat*, but since the Turks refused to let them pass, he suggested Vienna dispatch a French official to the front to act as courier. *Ibid.*, 430–31. For Wallis's defense on these questions, see *ibid.*, Appendices XIII–XV.

ramparts within six days of the signing of the agreement.[46] After allowing the secretaries two days to compose the final provisions, Neipperg and the grand vizier placed their signatures on the document on the morning of September 1, after which Villeneuve affixed the French guarantee.[47] Neipperg wrote to Wallis: "The peace is concluded and signed; stop all hostile action and cease firing; soon I will come to Belgrade."[48]

The first officer to greet Neipperg upon his return to Austrian positions was Schmettau, who scarcely believed what the plenipotentiary had done. The commandant of Belgrade simply refused to obey Neipperg's order to cease fire, pointing out lamely that, being a younger general of the artillery, the envoy had no authority to tell him what to do. A heated argument ensued, resolved only by the appearance of Wallis, who told Schmettau to accept Neipperg's commands.[49] Accordingly the shooting stopped, and on September 4 the first janissaries occupied the main portal and the supply depot of Belgrade. Two days later explosions marked the onset of the destruction of the fortifications.

The news of the surrender of Belgrade threw Vienna into despair and soon that despair turned to grief. Less than twenty-four hours after the messenger arrived with the draft of the treaty, another came with news of the greatest Russian victory of the war: the conquest of Khotin. By mid-August Münnich's forces had reached the environs of Khotin and there found a large Turkish army entrenched in the foothills of the Carpathian mountains. Once again confronted by the decision of risking his men in battle or returning to Russia

46 Constantine Dapontès, *Éphémérides Daces ou chronique de la guerre de quatre ans, 1736–1739* (Paris, 1881), II, 267.
47 Neipperg to emperor, September 2, 1739, in HHSA, SK, Türkei, 219.
48 Neipperg to Wallis, September 1, 1739, *ibid.*
49 Schmettau, *Mémoires secrets*, 262–63.

without a fight, this time Münnich chose to attack. Assaulting the Turkish positions with great gusto, the Russians crushed their foe in a pitched battle at Stavuchankh, forced the fortress garrison to flee Khotin, and, on September 14, ushered Münnich into Jassy, the capital of Turkish Moldavia, in triumph.[50]

The report of the great Russian success gave the Habsburg ministers a flicker of hope that they might nullify Neipperg's unfortunate settlement and, providing the Turkish tax continued and fresh troops arrived from Germany, press the war until the army could erase the Turkish threat to Belgrade. After all, the emperor could declare the treaty void on the grounds that the grand vizier had held Neipperg a virtual prisoner in his camp, and that Cagnoni's minor role in the discussions implied a separate Austro-Turkish peace—a condition expressly forbidden by Vienna.

But the real obstacle to abrogating the settlement and prolonging the struggle was the guarantee of the king of France. To repudiate the goodwill of Louis XV and Cardinal Fleury would constitute a diplomatic snub of major proportions, and Austria simply lacked the strength to pursue the conflict with the Ottoman Empire and weather a crisis with France. At a meeting on September 9 the Conference decided that, after publicly repudiating Neipperg, circulating explanations of his misconduct to the other European capitals, and apologizing to the Russians, the emperor must accept the treaty.[51] The war could not continue.

50 Manstein, *Contemporary Memoirs*, 223–26.
51 Konferenz Protokolle, September 9, 1739, and Bartenstein to emperor, September 13, 1739, in HHSA, SK, Vorträge, 49.

❦ Epilogue

Despite the conclusion of the preliminaries on September 1, the war had not officially ended, for all sides had to ratify the terms and compose a definitive settlement. Of foremost concern to Vienna was Russia's reaction to the preliminary articles. Although the empress' representative, Cagnoni, had authorized the agreement, St. Petersburg could argue that, given the hostile environment of the Turkish camp and possible intimidation exerted by Neipperg, Cagnoni had signed under pressure. Such a position would not only preclude Russian acceptance, but would also imply that Austria had effected a separate peace and thereby violated the convention of 1737. The final result of such a policy could be the dissolution of the Austro-Russian alliance and the alienation of France, which would hold Vienna responsible for Russia's noncompliance.

To encourage the empress' endorsement of the treaty and to avoid all the unwanted consequences of a rejection, Charles wrote her a personal letter on September 13 listing all the articles and apologizing for the behavior of his diplomats and military officers. Although his subordinates, especially Wallis and Neipperg, had acted entirely contrary to his orders and his intentions, the deed could not be undone because of the premature Turkish occupation of Belgrade and the French guarantee. In light of these regrettable circumstances, the emperor wrote, he could only accept the solution and plead with the empress to do the same.[1]

As one might expect, the initial Russian reaction to the report of the settlement and the emperor's letter was one of dismay. Upon hearing the news, Biron flew into a rage and refused to discuss the particulars until Cagnoni's explanation arrived. Ostermann, more composed than his colleague, was of the opinion that the emperor had made a bad peace at a bad time, but chose not to act until he received more information as to the details.[2] The most explosive response came from Münnich at Jassy, who wrote to Prince Lobkowitz, the Austrian commander in Transylvania:

> While the Russians take fortresses from the enemy, the Austrians raze or surrender them to him; while the Russians seize provinces, the Austrians give up whole kingdoms; while the Russians drive the foe to desperation, the Austrians grant him all he wishes, thereby flattering and encouraging his vanity; while the Russians continue the war, the Emperor signs an armistice and concludes peace. I ask what will become of that indissoluble alliance? I dare assure you, sir, that even had the Emperor's army been absolutely destitute, the Empress my sovereign would have secured for him a peace far more honorable than Vienna has obtained.[3]

Despite such vituperative comments, the Russians really had no choice but to accept the treaty, and at least Ostermann

1 Emperor to empress, September 13, 1739, in HHSA, SK, Russland, II, 140.
2 Botha to emperor, September 26, 1739, in *ibid.*, 20.
3 Münnich to Lobkowitz, September 13/24, 1739 in Brown, "Türkenkrieg," 1739, Appendix WWWW.

admitted it. Having just learned of negotiations for an accord between Sweden and the anti-Russian faction in Poland and Swedish plans to send 6,000 fully provisioned troops to Finland, the Russian foreign minister knew that, in the face of the mounting danger in the north and west, the war in the south must come to an end.[4] In fact, even before receiving the terms of the agreement of September 1, he had planned to restore newly conquered Khotin and all of Moldavia to the Turks if they would agree to stop fighting.[5] On October 3, therefore, Ostermann informed Botha on behalf of his sovereign that Russia would accept the Treaty of Belgrade.[6]

While St. Petersburg considered the terms, in Belgrade only the business of transforming the preliminaries into a definitive treaty remained. On September 18 Neipperg, Villeneuve, Cagnoni, and the grand vizier signed the formal document, whose most important provisions comprised the following: to the Turks went all of the Austrian possessions in Wallachia and Serbia, including the fortresses of Belgrade and Šabac with their fortifications intact (except, of course, those constructed at Belgrade since 1718) and the fortresses of New and Old Orsova with their bastions destroyed; the whole Banat remained in Austrian hands. The Russians and Turks agreed to raze Azov and create a no-man's land between the frontiers, the former being allowed to build a fortress north of Azov on the Don River and the latter one south on the Kuban. In exchange for promises never to restore its naval installation at Taganrog nor to permit its warships or

---

4 Botha to emperor, September 14, 1739, in HHSA, SK, Russland, II, 20. In early August, St. Petersburg mobilized its shore defenses when the red flag in the harbor signaled the approach of the Swedes. It proved to be a false alarm, however, for the warship turned out to be a Swedish merchant vessel. Botha to emperor, August 15, 1739, *ibid.*
5 Botha to emperor, September 25, 1739, *ibid.*
6 Botha to emperor, October 3, 1739, *ibid.*

commercial vessels to enter the Black Sea, St. Petersburg won for its merchants freedom of trade in the Ottoman Empire. Minor border questions went to a special commission for later resolution.[7] In December the emperor, empress, and sultan ratified the formal settlement, thus officially ending the war.

For the Habsburg Empire, the conclusion of the struggle had its immediate impact on the inhabitants of those lands lost to the Turks. The German colonists and those Serbs who preferred Austrian to Ottoman rule packed their possessions, collected their families, and crossed the Danube to find new homes and fields in imperial territory.[8] By June 8, 1740, the last Austrian troops evacuated Belgrade, and, as they left, one observer described the city: "Earlier one thought himself to be in Germany because the architecture, administration, commerce and manufacture, clothing, citizens, spirit, Christians, and Jews—all were German; and now: All European culture has disappeared, the city and its inhabitants have been devoured as if from earth and the city seems possessed by a foreign, Asiatic being." [9]

Regarding the army, troop strength still remained at a high level, almost 12,000 effectives from the garrison at Belgrade and 24,500 in the field forces, but provisions now had to be undertaken to move the soldiers to their regular quarters in Hungary and the Banat.[10] Among the officers and men, the most pressing concern remained the plague, and

7 For published copies of the Austro-Turkish and Russo-Turkish treaties, see Noradounghian, *Recueil d'actes internationaux*, I, 243–54, 258–65. The Russian, Austrian, and Turkish representatives met in Constantinople in the autumn of 1739 to settle the frontiers, but, because of the faulty language of the agreement of September 18, the Austro-Turkish debates lasted until May, 1741, and the Russo-Turkish discussions until August, 1741. Laugier, *Histoire des négociations*, II, 372–83.

8 Stefanović-Volovsky, *Belgrad unter der Regierung Karls VI*, 60.

9 Fritsch, *Paschas und Pest*, 52.

10 Brown, "Türkenkrieg," 1739, Appendix FFFF.

numerous precautions were instituted to lessen its impact when the forces encamped.[11] The army indeed had suffered minimal combat damage in this war, and, in spite of the plague, remained a formidable fighting force in southern Hungary.

Now that the fighting had ceased and the frantic negotiations concluded, the Conference in moments of reflection, decided that the sensational losses inflicted upon the venerable House of Habsburg necessitated some form of explanation to the courts of Europe. To combat the opinion that the empire suffered because of inherent weakness or collective incapacity, Vienna decided to place full responsibility for the misfortunes on Wallis and Neipperg. The former, the emperor wrote in a memorandum to all his ministers abroad, had contributed to Austria's defeat primarily through his military incompetence during and after Grocka. At the battle he refused to wait for necessary reinforcements (Neipperg's corps), attacked the enemy without adequate preparations, and ordered a retreat after winning the engagement; "at Grocka not the troops, but the leaders failed." Apparently not content with his blunders at Grocka, the report went on, the commander in chief then compounded his guilt a month later by allowing the Turks to occupy Belgrade without asking for instructions from Vienna. As for Neipperg, by surrendering Belgrade and then permitting the enemy to enter it before receiving official approval from the emperor, he "not only acted directly against his orders," but perpetrated a crime that had "no precedent in all of history." Having thus assigned the blame where thought due, the memorandum concluded by noting that, although strongly disapproving of the treaty, the emperor would accept it in deference to the guarantee of the king of France.[12]

11 *Ibid.*, 499 ff.
12 Emperor to all ministers, September 9, 1739, in HHSA, SK, Russland, II, 140.

After dispatching this circular, the conference imprisoned both Neipperg and Wallis and assigned Count John Harrach, the new president of the *Hofkriegsrat* and youngest brother of Count Aloysius Harrach, to head a commission to investigate their misconduct. The commission formulated forty-nine different accusations against Wallis, most of which concerned in various ways his inaction at the beginning of the campaign, his decisions to retreat after Grocka and Pančeva, and his refusal to allow communications to reach Neipperg in the Turkish camp; it drew up thirty-one charges against Neipperg, all related to his decisions while inspecting the army and negotiating the peace.[13] Despite the enormous amount of testimony accumulated by the board, it reached no decision because Maria Theresa abolished it upon her ascension to the throne and granted both officers full pardons. After Neipperg's release a rumor circulated that in August, 1739, while he negotiated with the Turks, he received a secret letter from Maria Theresa imploring him to abandon Belgrade so that she would not find herself at war with the Ottoman Empire upon the death of her father. No such letter existed, however, and indeed at that time Charles enjoyed such excellent health that his daughter had no premonition about ascending the throne in the near future.[14]

Now that the conflict had ended, the most important question involved the impact it would have on Austrian foreign policy, particularly toward the Ottoman Empire and Russia. As for Austrian affairs regarding the Ottoman Empire, the war of 1737–1739 really marked no noticeable change. De-

13 Brown, "Untersuchungsakten," 1739, Appendix 36, XI. For Neipperg's and Wallis' defenses, see Appendices 39, XIII–XV. In 1768 a commission reinvestigated the peacemaking with special attention to the roles of Gross and Neipperg. *Ibid.*, Appendix 40. An article based on the testimony of Wallis' hearing is Theodor Tupetz, "Der Türkenfeldzug von 1739 und der Friede zu Belgrad," *Historische Zeitschrift*, XL (1878), 1–51.

14 Regele, "Die Schuld des Grafen Neippergs," 390.

spite the surprising vigor displayed by the Turks, Vienna still looked upon the Ottoman state as woefully weak, and, should the emperor choose to fight the Turks in the future either for territorial gain or for some other reason, few Austrians believed the Ottomans would mount effective resistance. As Sinzendorf had remarked in early 1739, during the dark days of Austrian military misfortune, any peace with the Turks would be only temporary; and, as soon as the army and treasury had recovered, the empire, if it wished, could again expand its influence into the Balkans.[15]

Regarding Russia, throughout the struggle relations between the two powers had been strained, and it would seem that the terrible disappointment and frustrations of the peace treaty would surely dissolve the Austro-Russian alliance. But the alliance did not dissolve; indeed soon after the signing, both Vienna and St. Petersburg expressed the wish to maintain it. On September 29, 1739, only a month after the settlement, Sinzendorf advised the emperor: "We must work extremely hard, not only to put us in a good light, but to create a clearer and better concert with Russia." [16] Two weeks later Bartenstein reported that, in a meeting of the Conference: "First and foremost it was unanimously recognized that Russia, the only ally which up until now has demonstrated its loyalty, must be retained, and most of the talk focused on the necessity of the Russian alliance, not only for the present, but for the future." [17]

Even before Vienna had announced its wish to continue the association with St. Petersburg, on October 3 Ostermann had revealed a like desire when he told Botha that he "hoped His Imperial Majesty, despite what had happened at Belgrade,

15 Konferenz Protokolle, February 4, 1739, in HHSA, SK, Vorträge, 48.
16 Sinzendorf to emperor, September 29, 1739, *ibid.*, 49.
17 Bartenstein to emperor, October 17, 1739, *ibid.*

would continue his friendship and alliance with the Empress."
Admittedly St. Petersburg's need appeared more immediate
than Vienna's, for it still feared an attack from Sweden and
Poland. Ostermann expressed this concern by asking the
emperor "as soon as possible to turn the greatest attention
toward maintaining peace in the north." [18] Whatever the reasons, in December, 1739, Austria and Russia issued a joint
declaration of "indissoluble alliance" and a renewal of the
treaty of 1726.[19]

Whereas Russia's motives for continuing the pact appeared
quite understandable, the reasons behind Vienna's devotion
to the accord did not seem so clear. Indeed Russia had remained loyal throughout the past struggle, but its repeated
uncooperativeness regarding strategy and war aims, the suf-
ferings the Austrians felt they endured because of that uncooperativeness, and the frequent outbursts of animosity
between individuals on both sides might indicate that Vienna
would become noticeably cooler toward St. Petersburg in the
future. At this particular moment, however, the European
scene had again changed so that the Conference still regarded
the Russian accord the most important element in its diplomatic maneuvering. After 1736, if any power would replace
Russia as Austria's foremost partner, it would likely be
France. Not only had Cardinal Fleury continuously voiced
his friendship during the negotiations leading to the final
conclusion of the War of the Polish Succession, but Paris'
recognition of the Pragmatic Sanction and refusal to support
the Ottoman Empire diplomatically in the War of 1737–
1739 only confirmed the approaching rapprochement between
the two continental powers. Furthermore, by refusing to aid
Vienna in either the Polish or the Turkish war and by en-

---

18 Botha to emperor, October 3, 1739, in *ibid.*, Russland, II, 20.
19 Martens, *Recueil des traités*, I, 126–27.

gaging in hostilities with Spain in 1739, Britain seemed no longer interested in restoring its old association with the House of Habsburg.

In 1739 the growing unity between Paris and Vienna collapsed, however, both because of France's mediation in the unfortunate peace treaty—whose results many Austrians and non-Austrians attributed to the influence of Villeneuve—and because Fleury had included Prussia in his northern system to put pressure on Russia.[20] Vienna in 1739 considered no power more dangerous to its interests than Prussia and mistrusted any state that made Berlin its friend.[21] Because Paris had now reached an agreement with Prussia, the only remaining power that could keep Frederick William inactive, the Conference believed, was again the old Habsburg ally, Russia.[22] Russia had helped Austria against France in 1733–1735, against Turkey in 1737–1739, and hopefully would do so against Prussia at some future date; in the autumn of 1739, therefore, the accord with St. Petersburg had once again become the most convenient for Austria's general European interests.[23]

Curiously the very crisis for which Vienna had retained the Russian union occurred in the year following the Treaty of Belgrade, when Frederick II of Prussia launched his assault on the Austrian province of Silesia. At that critical moment, when Austria needed its ally most, its old associates in the Russian capital displayed a remarkable coolness towards Vienna's pleas for help. Arguing that St. Petersburg

20 Braubach, *Versailles und Wien*, 331.
21 Bartenstein to emperor, October 15, 1739, in HHSA, SK, Vorträge, 49.
22 Emperor to Botha and Hohenholz, November 8, 1739, *ibid.*, Russland, II, 141.
23 Martens, *Recueil des traités*, I, 145–76. For a brief discussion of Austria's eastern policy at this time, see Walter Leitsch, "Die Ostpolitik Kaiser Karls VI," *Veröffentlichungen des Verbändes österreichischer Geschichts-vereine*, XI (1957), 150–57.

should wait developments, complaining of Austria's performance in the Turkish war, and calling attention to a possible war with Sweden, Empress Anne and her advisers refused to honor their obligations. Before Vienna could protest this policy, the Russian sovereign died and St. Petersburg itself fell into a succession crisis of its own that precluded all Austrian hopes of aid from their allies.

Although this policy threatened to end Astro-Russian harmony for some time to come, the Prussian menace and the convenience of the Russian union remained, therefore, swallowing any ill-feelings, the Austrians restored the alliance in 1746 to fight Frederick II.[24] Although intense fighting did not begin until ten years later, when hostilities did erupt the union emerged as the one solid concord in the famous reversal of alliances which set the stage for the Seven Years' War. For a century after this major European dispute, Austro-Russian cooperation remained a common feature of diplomacy, spanning the Polish partitions, the Turkish war of 1787–1791, the wars of the French Revolution, and the famous years of the Holy Alliance and the Metternich era. Not until the Crimean War did the concordat suffer a serious blow, and even for decades afterward Vienna and St. Petersburg preferred to reach common understandings rather than resort to arms to solve problems of mutual interest. In fact in all their history, the Habsburg and Romanovs did not cross swords in earnest until the great war of 1914–1918, a war that brought down both their houses.

Austrian policy in the war of 1737–1739 marked the first time that a power appreciated the potential of Russia as a decisive influence in European affairs. Before 1730 the Russian colossus had made a minor imprint on western foreign

24 For a discussion of the treaty of 1746, see Paul Karge, *Die russisch-österreichische Allianz von 1746 und ihre Vorgeschichte* (Göttingen, 1886).

relations; by 1739 it had become so important that the prestigious House of Habsburg made substantial sacrifices to maintain its loyalty. Despite the haphazard diplomacy, the mismanaged military effort, and the at times inept analysis of affairs, one could argue that Vienna correctly judged the importance of Russia in Europe, and, by making that judgment and securing Russia as its friend, achieved success for its future.

✣ Bibliography

1. PRIMARY SOURCES

A. Manuscript

Vienna: Haus- Hof- und Staatsarchiv:
Staatskanzlei:
    Vorträge, Konferenz-Protokolle, Referate—Kartonen 42–49.
    Russland, Neuere Akten II—Kartonen 13–20, 128–41,
        206, 210, 212–13, 221, 224, 228–29, 235, 242.
    Türkei—Kartonen 211–20.
    Kriegsakten—Fascikel 324.
Reichskanzlei:
    Russland, Neuere Akten—Kartonen 32–34.
Vienna: Kriegsarchiv:
Brown, Johann Georg. "Türkenkrieg, welcher im Jahr 1737
    angefangen und im Jahr 1739 mit dem Belgrader Frieden
    sich geendiget hat." 5 vols.
    ————. "Untersuchungsakten über General Doxat, FM Graf von
    Seckendorf, FM Graf Wallis, und FZM Graf Neipperg."
    4 vols.

B. Printed

D'Argenson, Marquis de. *Journal and Memoirs.* 2 vols. Boston,
    1901.
Arneth, Alfred von (ed.). "Eigenhändige Correspondenz des
    Königs von Spanien (nachmals Kaiser Karl VI) mit dem
    Obersten Kanzler des Königreiches Böhmen, Grafen Johann

Bibliography 185

Wenzel Wratislaw." *Archiv für österreichische Geschichte*, XVI (1856).

—— (ed.). "Die Relationen des Botschafter Venedigs über Österreich im achtzehnten Jahrhundert." *Fontes rerum Austriacarum*, Series 2, XXII (1863), 1–351.

Bell, John. *Travels from St. Petersburg in Russia to Various Parts of Asia.* Edinburgh, 1806.

Dapontès, Constantine. *Éphémérides Daces ou chronique de la querre de quatre ans, 1736–1739.* 3 vols. Paris, 1881.

Friedrich Wilhelm I. *Die Briefe König Friedrich Wilhelms I an den Fürsten Leopold zu Anhalt-Dessau, 1704–1740.* Berlin, 1905.

Fritsch, Gerhard. *Paschas und Pest.* Graz and Vienna, 1962.

Hantsch, Hugo. "Die drei grossen Relationen St. Saphorins über die inneren Verhältnisse am Wiener Hof zur Zeit Karls VI." *Mitteilungen des Instituts für österreichische Geschichte*, LVIII (1950), 625–36.

Hurmuzaki, Eudoxius, Baron von. *Fragmente zur Geschichte de Rumänen.* 5 vols. Bucharest, 1878–86.

Kallbrunner, Josef (ed.). *Kaiserin Maria Theresias politisches Testament.* Vienna, 1952.

De Ligne, Prince Charles. *Mélanges militaires, littéraires, et sentimentaires.* 28 vols. Leopoldberg, 1795–1805.

Manstein, Christoph Hermann von. *Contemporary Memoirs of Russia, 1727–1744.* London, 1968.

Martens, F. *Recueil des traités et conventions conclus par la Russe avec les puissances étrangères.* 13 vols. St. Petersburg, 1874–1902.

Moser, Johann Jacob. *Der Belgradische Friedens-schluss zwischen Ihro Römische-kayserl. Majestät und der ottomanischen Pforte.* Jena, 1740.

Münnich, Burchard Christoph von. "Tagebuch über den ersten Feldzug des in den Jahren 1735–1739 geführten russisch-türkischen Krieges." Ernst Hermann (ed). *Beiträge zur Geschichte des russischen Reiches.* Leipzig, 1843. 117–243.

Noradounghian, Gabriel. *Recueil d'actes internationaux de l'empire Ottoman, 1300–1789.* Paris, 1897.

Pollnitz, Charles Lewis. *Memoirs.* 4 vols. London, 1739–1740.

Recueil des instructions données aux ambassadeurs et ministères de France depuis des traités de Westphalie jusqu'à la revolution francaise. 25 vols. Paris, 1884–1929.

Saussure, César de. *Lettres de Turquie, 1730–1739, et notices, 1740.* Budapest, 1909.

Sbornik Russkago Istoricheskago Obshchestva, Collections of the

Russian Historical Society. 148 vols. St. Petersburg, 1867–
    1916.
Schmettau, Count de. *Mémoires secrets de la querre de Hongrie*
    (*pendant les campagnes de 1737, 1738, et 1739*). Frank-
    furt, 1786.

2. SECONDARY MATERIALS

A. *Books*

Abeken, Hermann. *Der Eintritt der Türkei in die europäische
    Politik des achtzehnten Jahrhunderts.* Berlin, 1856.
Arneth, Alfred von. *Geschichte Maria Theresia's.* 10 vols. Vi-
    enna, 1863–79.
———. *Prinz Eugen von Savoyen.* 3 vols. Vienna, 1864.
Bain, R. Nisbet. *The Pupils of Peter the Great.* New York, 1899.
Benedikt, Heinrich. *Der Pascha-Graf Alexander von Bonneval,
    1675–1747.* Graz, 1959.
Bittner, Ludwig. *Chronologisches Verzeichnis der österreichi-
    schen Staatsverträge.* 4 vols. Vienna, 1903–17.
Bourgeois, Emile. *Le secret des Farnèse.* Paris, 1909.
———. *Le secret du régent et la politique de l'abbé Dubois.* Paris,
    1909.
Braubach, Max. *Geschichte und Abenteuer: Gestalten um den
    Prinzen Eugen.* Munich, 1950.
———. *Prinz Eugen von Savoyen.* 5 vols. Munich, 1963–65.
———. *Versailles und Wien von Ludwig XIV bis Kaunitz.* Bonn,
    1952.
Brückner, A. *Die Familie Braunschweig in Russland im achtzehn-
    ten Jahrhundert.* St. Petersburg, 1876.
Cassels, Lavender. *The Struggle for the Ottoman Empire, 1717–
    1740.* London, 1966.
D'Elvert, Christian. *Zur österreichischen Verwaltungs-Geschichte
    mit besonderer Rücksicht auf die böhmischen Länder.* Brno,
    1880.
Droysen, Johann Gustav. *Geschichte der preussischen Politik.* 5
    parts. Vol. IV, Pts. 3 and 4. Berlin, 1855–86.
Frederick the Great. *Histoire de mon temps.* Berlin, 1846.
———. *Mémoires pour servir à l'histoire de la maison de Brande-
    bourg.* 2 vols. Berlin, 1846.
Hammer-Purgstall, Joseph von. *Geschichte des osmanischen
    Reiches.* 10 vols. Pest, 1827–35.
Hausmann, Friedrich. *Repertorium der diplomatischen Vertreter
    aller Länder.* 2 vols. Zurich, 1950.
Hempel, Christian Friedrich. *Leben, Thaten, und berümbter Fall*

des weltberufenen russischen Grafen Burchards Christophs von Münnich. Bremen, 1743.

Hennings, Fred. *Und sitzet zur linken Hand: Franz Stephan von Lothringen.* Vienna, 1961.

Horn, David Bayne. *Great Britain and Europe in the Eighteenth Century.* Oxford, 1967.

Kallbrunner, Josef. *Das kaiserliche Banat: Einrichtung und Entwicklung des Banats bis 1739.* Munich, 1958.

Karge, Paul. *Die russisch-österreichische Allianz von 1746 und ihre Vorgeschichte.* Göttingen, 1886.

Keralio, [?], M. de. *Histoire de la guerre des Russes et des Impériaux contre les Turcs.* 2 vols. Paris, 1780.

Király, Béla. *Hungary in the Late Eighteenth Century.* New York, 1969.

La Lande, [?]. *Histoire de l'empereur Charles VI.* 6 vols. The Hague, 1743.

Laugier, M. l'Abbé. *Histoire des négociations pour la paix conclue à Belgrade, le 18 septembre 1739.* 2 vols. Paris, 1768.

Leitsch, Walter. *Moskau und die Politik des Kaiserhofes im XVII Jahrhundert, 1604–1654.* Graz, 1960.

Lockhart, L. *Nadir Shah.* London, 1938.

Marczali, Henry. *Hungary in the Eighteenth Century.* Cambridge, Eng., 1910.

Mayer, F. M. *Die Anfänge des Handels und der Industrie in Österreich und die Orientalische Compagnie.* Innsbruck, 1882.

Mediger, Walther. *Moskaus Weg nach Europa.* Braunschweig, 1952.

Mensi, Franz von. *Die Finanzen Österreichs von 1701 bis 1740.* Vienna, 1890.

Meynert, Hermann. *Geschichte des Kriegswesens und der Heeresverfassung in den verschiedenen Ländern der österreichischen Monarchie.* 3 vols. Vienna, 1852–54.

Mikoletzky, Hanns Leo. *Österreich: Das grosse 18. Jahrhundert.* Munich and Vienna, 1967.

Muret, Pierre. *La prépondérance anglaise, 1715–1763.* Paris, 1949.

Picot, Emile. *Les Serbes de Hongrie.* Prague, 1873.

Plumb, J. H. *Sir Robert Walpole.* 2 vols. London, 1956–60.

Przezdziecki, Renaud. *Diplomatie et protocole à la cour de Pologne.* 2 vols. Paris, 1934–37.

Redlich, Oswald. *Das Werden einer Grossmacht: Österreich von 1700 bis 1740.* Vienna, 1962.

Regele, Oskar. *Das österreichische Hofkriegsrat, 1556–1848.* Vienna, 1949.

Rothenberg, Gunther Erich. *The Austrian Military Border in Croatia, 1522–1747.* Urbana, 1960.

_____. *The Military Border in Croatia, 1740–1881.* Chicago, 1966.

Sautai, Maurice. *Les préliminaires de la querre de la succession d'Autriche.* Paris, 1907.

Sax, Carl von. *Geschichte des Machtverfalls der Türkei.* Vienna, 1908.

Shay, Mary Lucille. *The Ottoman Empire from 1720 to 1734 as Revealed in the Despatches of the Venetian Baili.* Urbana, 1944.

Soloviev, Sergei Makhailovich., *Istoriia Rossii s Drevneishikh Vremen.* 15 vols. Moscow, 1959–66.

Stavenow, Ludwig. *Geschichte Schwedens, 1718–1772.* Gotha, 1908.

Stefanović-Volovsky, Theodore von. *Belgrad unter der Regierung Kaiser Karls VI, 1717–1739.* Vienna, 1908.

Uebersberger, Hans. *Österreich und Russland seit dem Ende des 15. Jahrhunderts.* Vienna and Leipzig, 1906.

_____. *Russlands Orientpolitik in den letzten zwei Jahrhunderten.* Stuttgart, 1913.

Vandal, Albert. *Une ambassade française en Orient sous Louis XV: La mission du Marquis de Villeneuve, 1728–1741.* Paris, 1887.

Vaucher, Paul. *Robert Walpole et la politique de Fleury, 1731–1742.* Paris, 1924.

Waliszewski, K. *L'héritage de Pierre le grand: Règne des femmes, gouvernement des favoris, 1725–1741.* Paris, 1900.

Walter, Friedrich. *Die Paladine der Kaiserin.* Vienna, 1959.

Wilson, Arthur McCandless. *French Foreign Policy during the Administration of Cardinal Fleury, 1726–1743.* Cambridge, Mass., 1936.

Wittram, Reinhard. *Peter I: Czar und Kaiser.* 2 vols. Göttingen, 1964.

Wrede, Alphons von. *Geschichte der k. und k. Wehrmacht.* 5 vols. Vienna, 1898–1905.

Zeller, Gaston. *Les temps modernes: De Louis XIV à 1789.* Paris, 1955.

Zimmermann, Jürg. *Militärverwaltung und Heeresaufbringung in Österreich bis 1806.* Vol. I, Pt. 3 of *Handbuch zur deutschen Militärgeschichte.* Militärgeschichtliches Forschungsamt (ed.). Bundesrepublik Deutschlands. Frankfurt a/M, 1965.

Zinkeisen, Johann Wilhelm. *Geschichte des osmanischen Reiches in Europa.* 7 vols. Gotha, 1840–63.

B. *Magazines*

A. [Angeli, Moriz von]. "Marginalien zu dem Aufsätze 'Nikolaus Doxat, ein Officer des Prinzen Eugenius und ein Opfer des damaligen Hofkriegsrathes.' " *Mitteilungen des k. k. Kriegsarchivs,* (1881), 239–46.

Angeli, Moriz von. "Der Krieg mit der Pforte, 1736 bis 1739." *Mitteilungen des k. k. Kriegsarchivs,* (1881), 247–338, 409–79.

Arneth, Alfred von. "Johann Christoph Bartenstein und seine Zeit." *Archiv für österreichische Geschichte,* XLVI (1871), 3–214.

Beer, Adolph. "Zur Geschichte der Politik Karls VI." *Historische Zeitschrift,* LV (1886), 1–70.

Benedikt, Heinrich. "Die europäische Politik der Pforte vor Beginn und während des österreichischen Erbfolgekrieges." *Mitteilungen des österreichischen Staatsarchivs,* I (1948), 137–92.

Beyrich, Rudolf. "Kursachsen und die polnische Thronfolge, 1733–1736," *Leipziger historische Abhandlungen,* XXXVI (1913), 1–64.

Braubach, Max. "Johann Christoph Bartensteins Herkunft und Anfänge," *Mitteilungen des Instituts für österreichische Geschichtsforschung,* LXI (1953), 45–140.

———. "Eine Satire auf den Wiener Hof aus den letzten Jahren Kaiser Karls VI." *Mitteilungen des Instituts für österreichische Geschichtsforschung,* LIII (1934), 21–78.

Brunner, Otto. "Das Haus Österreich und die Donaumonarchie." Hellmuth Rössler (ed.). *Festgabe dargebracht Harold Steinacker.* Munich, 1955. 122–44.

Frauenholz, E. von. "Prinz Eugen und die kaiserliche Armee." *Münchener historische Abhandlungen,* II, Pt. 1 (1932), 1–14.

Hrazky, Josef. "Johann Christoph Bartenstein der Staatsmann und Erzieher." *Mitteilungen des österreichischen Staatsarchivs,* XI (1958), 221–51.

Krones, F. "Zur Geschichte Ungarns im Zeitalter Franz Rákóczis II." Pt. 2. *Archiv für österreichische Geschichte,* XLIII (1870), 1–102.

Langer, Johann. "Nord-Albaniens und der Herzegowina Unter-
werfungs-Anerbieten an Österreich, 1737–1739." *Archiv
für österreichische Geschichte*, LXII (1881), 239–304.
Leitsch, Walter. "Die Ostpolitik Kaiser Karls VI." *Veröffent-
lichungen des Verbändes österreichischer Geschichtsvereine*,
XI (1957), 150–57.
_____. "Der Wandel der österreichischen Russlandpolitik in den
Jahren 1724–1726." *Jahrbücher für Geschichte Osteuropas*,
VI (1958), 33–91.
Puttkamer, Ellinor von. "Frankreich, Russland, und der polnische
Thron, 1733." *Osteuropäische Forschungen*, N.F., XXIV
(1937), 1–116.
Redlich, Oswald. "Die Tagebücher Kaiser Karls VI." *Gesamt-
deutsche Vergangenheit: Festgabe für Heinrich Ritter von
Srbik*. Munich, 1938. 141–51.
Regele, Oskar. "Die Schuld des Grafen Reinhard Wilhelm von
Neippergs am Belgrader Frieden, 1739, und an der Nieder-
lage bei Mollwitz, 1741." *Mitteilungen des österreichischen
Staatsarchivs*, VII (1954), 373–98.
Spuler, Bertold. "Die europäische Diplomatie in Konstantinopel
bis zum Frieden von Belgrad." *Jahrbücher für Kultur und
Geschichte der Slaven*, XI (1935), 53–115, 171–222.
Stix, Franz. "Zur Geschichte und Organisation der Wiener ge-
heimen Ziffernkanzlei (von ihren Anfängen bis zum Jahre
1848)." *Mitteilungen des Instituts für österreichische Ge-
schichtsforschung* LI (1937), 131–60.
Stoye, John. "Emperor Charles VI: The Early Years of His
Reign." *Transactions of the Royal Historical Society*. 5th
ser., XII (1962), 63–84.
Tupetz, Theodor. "Der Türkenfeldzug von 1739 und der Friede
zu Belgrad." *Historische Zeitschrift*, XL (1878), 1–51.
Vucinich, Wayne S. "The Serbs in Austria-Hungary." *Austrian
History Yearbook*, III (1967), Pt. 2, 3–47.

৪৯ Index

Albania: as possible Austrian war aim, 64

Amalia, empress mother, 15

Anne, empress of Russia: background, 39; and advisers, 40–42; defends Ostermann, 129; marriage of niece, 149–50; mentioned, 182

Augustus II, king of Poland and Elector of Saxony: death of, 36; threat to Austria, 37; mentioned, 45, 46

Augustus III: character, 46; election as king of Poland, 47; and kingship, 49; rejection of Russian request to cross Polish land, 148; mentioned, 83

Austria:
—army: financial needs of, 15; colonels of regiments, 18–19; irregularities in, 19–20; recruitment, 19–20; artillery, 21; cavalry, 21; strength of, 23, 135, 157, 176–77; condition of, 48, 52, 56–57, 94–99, 135, 139, 176–77. *See also* Hofkriegsrat
—court, high cost of: 15
—foreign policy: and Russia, 32, 34–36, 49–50; and Spain, 34; and Ottoman Empire, 34–35, 44–45, 59–61; general, 35, 36, 48; and Poland, 37, 39. *See also* Privy Conference; Bartenstein, John Christopher
—state debt, 17. *See also* Hofkammer

Austrian Netherlands (Belgium), 3

Azov, fortress of: as Russian war aim, 59, 65, 88; Russian conquest of, 69; Russian willingness to surrender, 152–53; mentioned, 130, 163, 175

Babadag, village of: as Ottoman headquarters, 42, 75, 87

Bakhchisaray: sack of, 70

Banat of Timişoara (Temesvar), 4–7 *passim*, 161, 164, 175, 176

Banja Luka, battle of, 110

Barcelona, 7

Barenklau, John Leopold: assigned to negotiate strategy with Russians, 77; description of Ochakov, 106–107, 108; mentioned, 78, 79, 109

191

47; and Austria, 82; mentioned, 36

Starhemberg, Gundaker Thomas: character, 12; advocate of war, 56, 66, 100; warns of worsening conditions, 153; mentioned, 11, 30

Stavuchankh, battle of, 172

Succow, General, 165

Sweden: possible enemy of Russia, 44, 122, 132, 144–45; subsidy treaty with France, 145

Talman, Leopold: appointed ambassador, 62; Ostermann's disapproval of, 63; proposed campaign plan, 75–76; and Austrian policy, 83–85; and Königsegg, 86–87, 91–92; appointment as mediator, 87; as mediator, 89, 90; at Nemirov, 104, 109, 112; mentioned, 44, 64

Tartars. *See* Crimean Tartars

Theil, Nicholas, 118–19

Timişoara, fortress of: threatened by Turks, 141; mentioned, 7, 157, 163

Transylvania: Russian expeditionary corps to, 143–45, 148–49; mentioned, 3, 77, 79, 113

Treaty of 1726: provisions of, 32; causes for, 32–34; and Britain, 32–34. *See also* Austria, foreign policy; Russia, foreign policy

Turkish tax (*Türkensteuer*), 16, 172

Turkish war, 1716–18, p. 4

Uzice, fortress of: conquered by Turks, 137

Venice: as potential Austrian ally, 83

Vidin, fortress of: as part of Talman's plan, 76; as Austrian objective, 76–77, 108–109;

mentioned, 99, 101, 110, 111, 137

Vienna, siege of (1683), 3

Vienna, Treaty of, 1725: and Britain, 32–33; mentioned, 27–28

Villeneuve, Marquis: invested by Turks with peace-making powers, 154; and Treaty of Belgrade, 167, 168, 169, 171, 175, 181; mentioned, 82, 121, 129, 153, 163

Vishniakov, Alexei: and Turkey, 42; protests Tartar march, 51; mentioned, 63

Volinsky, Artemus: as Russian negotiator at Nemirov, 90

Wager, Charles, 33–34

Wallachia (Austrian or Litle Wallachia): invaded by Turks, 1738, p. 137; mentioned, 4, 153, 175

Wallachia (Turkish): as Russian war aim, 59–60, 72, 106, 107–108, 116; Habsburg interest in, 65; as Austrian war aim, 108; scene of fighting, 111; mentioned, 74, 76, 99, 101, 113, 120

Wallis, Oliver: character, 155; and strategy for campaign of 1739, pp. 156–58; at Grocka, 160–61; and campaign of 1739, pp. 164–66; and Schmettau, 165–66; and Treaty of Belgrade, 168, 170, 171, 173; charges against, 177–78; mentioned, 76n

Walpole, Horatio: speculates on Austrian belligerence, 80; and Russian war aims, 125n

Walpole, Robert: and British avoidance of war, 1733, p. 48

Wolfenbüttel (duchy): contribution to war effort, 1737, pp. 23, 96

Württemberg, Alexander, 4

Zenta, battle of, 1697, p. 116